"Both my girls were practically grown and gone the first time I discovered Meg Meeker's *Strong Fathers, Strong Daughters*, but it still had a huge impact on how I talk to and relate with them. *Strong Fathers, Strong Daughters: The 30-Day Challenge* is the book I wish someone had given me the day my first daughter was born!"

—DAVE RAMSEY
New York Times bestselling author,
nationally syndicated radio show host,
and father of two daughters

"Meg Meeker radically changed the way I look at parenting and fatherhood. There is joy, wisdom, and truth in everything she writes, and I will be the first in line to buy each new book she shares with the world."

—JON ACUFF
Wall Street Journal bestselling author of
*Quitter: Closing the Gap Between
Your Day Job & Your Dream Job* and
father of two daughters

"Raising four daughters while playing professional football was very demanding. Dr. Meeker is oh-so-accurate when she points out just how observant and impressionable young girls can be! Her work always inspires me to do a better job, and *The 30-Day Challenge* is filled with lots of good ideas. Thanks, Meg!"

—CHRIS GODFREY
father of six, member of New York Giants
Super Bowl XXI Championship Team,
estate planning attorney and
president of Life Athletes

"Dads need help, particularly when it comes to building bonds with their daughters. Dr. Meeker's wise, practical book offers fathers activities they can do today to establish a relationship with their daughters that will extend far into the future. Get this book now and spare your family and your daughter the mistakes that so many men have made in the past."

—Raymond Arroyo
New York Times bestselling author,
host of EWTN's *The World Over*

Strong Fathers, Strong Daughters

The 30-Day Challenge

By Meg Meeker, M.D.

Author of

Strong Fathers, Strong Daughters:
10 Secrets Every Father Should Know

The A Group
320 Seven Springs Way
Suite 100
Brentwood, TN 37027

For information on ordering copies of this book, contact The A Group at (866) 258-4800 or
by email at info@agroup.com.

Printed in the United States of America

ISBN: 978-0-9836620-2-0

*This book is dedicated to
my beloved father, Wally.*

Contents

SECRETS
EVERY
FATHER
SHOULD
KNOW

SECRET 1

You Are the Most Important Man in Her Life

You are the filter through which your daughter processes her beliefs about all other men, even God. This week, be courageous enough to examine what kind of a filter you are.

Do you give men a good name, or are you showing her that men are scary, disinterested, and aloof?

Your Speech
- What is your tone like?
- Are you critical or encouraging?

Your Presence
- Daughters want their fathers to move closer to them, not farther away.
- What are you doing to grow closer to your daughter?

Read the Introduction and Chapter One, "You Are the Most Important Man in Her Life," in Strong Fathers, Strong Daughters.

Day One

The Daddy Template

Here's a thought that will make your hair stand on end: You, Dad, are a template for all male figures—teachers, boyfriends, her husband, uncles, and even God himself—in your daughter's life. Because you are there from her earliest years, you set a template over your daughter's mind and heart regarding how she will interact with all males. If you are kind, she will expect all males to be kind. If you are harsh and critical, then she will expect the same treatment from other men.

Being a template is an extraordinary responsibility and is sobering. But you can handle it. You are a man. You are wired with everything you need in order to be a great dad.

You may be living at this moment with evidence of the truth about fathers being a template in their daughters' lives. How is your wife or girlfriend relating to you? Does she have difficulty trusting you without good reason? Does she ever get angry with you over things that you didn't do? If the answer is *yes*, you may have a bone to pick with her dear-old dad. The truth is, because daughters watch their dads so intensely, they learn about maleness and masculinity from you. They don't just watch how you treat them; they watch how you treat their mothers. One of the best gifts that a father can give his daughter is to treat her mother with respect and love. Your daughter gets clues about how her husband should treat her.

So be very, very careful. If you have a strong marriage, show her mother affection. If you have a rocky one, continue to take the high road. Don't criticize her mother in front of her and most certainly, get your anger under control. Angry men are terrifying to daughters. You can show love to her, but if she sees your anger erupt at her mother, she will be frightened of you nonetheless.

When You Are Divorced

Perhaps you have been through a tough divorce, and her mother is pitting your daughter against you. Though it requires a great deal of courage, insist on being respectful toward her mother. In doing so, you do your daughter an enormous and life-changing service. You teach her that even when men are under duress, she should expect them to treat her well.

I hear from men every week who feel estranged from their daughters by angry mothers. They ask me what they should do to keep their relationships with their daughters strong. Here's what they need to know: Daughters always return to what is right and good. If you keep your wits about you and act like a good, loving man, refusing to get caught up in wars with her mother, she will come back to you. Maybe she will stay detached as a teen, but when she matures and enters her adult years, she will be drawn to your integrity and want a relationship with you. Hold on.

> One of the best gifts that a father can give his daughter is to treat her mother with respect and love.

What Is God Like?

Little girls tell me wonderful things. One young first grader, Carrie, chatted with me about God one day. Curious to know her perceptions of God, I asked Carrie, "So what do you think God is like?"

"Oh, that's easy," she said. "He's got real brown hair and a mustache on his lip. And he's really quiet and nice." I watched her mother smile.

"Do you ever talk to God?" I continued.

"Yup. Kinda a lot. He likes me. If I could see him, I would like to sit on his lap and tell him secrets. He is so big and squishy, and he listens a lot."

Carrie's mother pulled out a photo of her dad who was serving time in the military. He had dark brown hair, a mustache, and a quiet looking demeanor. I couldn't tell whether or not he was squishy, but I imagine he was.

Day One Challenge: Give Her More of You

Tell your daughter stories about your childhood. She will enjoy learning more about you and will readily identify with your stories about life when you were her age.

Checklist

O Think about specific events in your childhood and growing up years. To help jog your memory, write some brief answers to these questions:

- What's your earliest memory?

- What's the funniest, most embarrassing, or most scary moment you can recall?

- Who was your best friend and what were some adventures the two of you had together?

- What extracurricular activities did you enjoy doing?

O Determine a time when you'll share your childhood stories with your daughter.

O Put it on the calendar!

Day Two

With the Eyes of a Hawk

The moment you walk into a room, your daughter knows that you are there. She tunes into you because she needs to figure a few things out. Do you see her? Do you like what she is wearing? Are you mad at her? Do you approve of what she is doing at that moment? She needs to answer these questions not because she is really concerned about you; she is concerned about herself. Developmentally, she is very egocentric. She watches you with the eyes of a hawk because she wants to feel better. And finding out some things about you will help her accomplish this.

Remember, your daughter is tied to you. You may leave the house and return without thinking about her, but she can't do this. She is trying to figure out life, who she is, and where she "fits" into the bigger scheme of things all day long—whether you are with her or away from her. And you are integral to this process. Your presence and behaviors center her.

Seeking Your Approval

Even when you aren't paying attention, your daughter is reading you and making decisions about herself. This is a simple truth about her life that you need to know, but don't let it frighten you. Her identity is forming, and much of it relates to what she sees in you. Since she doesn't know who she is, she watches you to figure herself out. If she sees you respond positively to what she is drawing, reading, or accomplishing, then she will realize that she is capable of succeeding at her work. If she believes that you see her as smart, strong, and independent, she will become these things. Your responses to her speech and behaviors form an image in her mind and then she internalizes those images and "tries them on."

Daughters do this to some extent with their mothers, but they do so differently. In her eyes, you carry an authority with a capital A. What you think and believe carries weight in her mind. If she feels that you approve of her, as she matures, this authority stays strong. If she feels constantly disappointed and hurt, your influence stays strong, but it works in reverse. She begins to internalize pain, and that pain will feel magnified even as she matures. So for good or ill, whether you make her stronger or cause her reason to hurt, her impressions of your responses to her become seared onto her heart like a giant tattoo.

Make Her Feel Smart and Important

When Allie was six years old, her engineer father began taking her to work with him on Saturday mornings. While he made phone calls, she would sit at his desk and spin in his enormous leather chair. When I spoke to her, now thirty-six, she could still recall the smell of the leather, she said. After several hours at the office, she and her father would leave and walk to a nearby deli to have lunch. Every Saturday they continued this routine until she was in her early teens.

"Being there with my dad made me feel smart. I don't remember my dad telling me I was smart, but somehow I just knew that he believed that I was. Being with him in his huge office while he conducted his work made me feel like I was a part of it all. That's what made me feel good, I guess, that my dad thought that I could enter in. As I got older, he would ask me questions about things—important things. I know he didn't heed any of my advice, but he asked and that's what made me feel important."

If she believes that you see her as smart, strong, and independent, she will become these things.

Today, Allie runs a very successful engineering business. She has a beautiful office and a large leather chair at her desk.

Day Two Challenge: Teach Her Something

What skills do you possess that you can teach to your daughter? Maybe you can teach her to master the guitar, play tennis, or change the oil in the car. As she learns at your side, she'll more closely identify with you.

Checklist

○ Gather what you'll need for lessons with your daughter.

○ Set aside time for the teaching and learning. Put it on the calendar!

○ Encourage your daughter to practice her new skill.

Day Three

Daddy to the End

Every woman takes one man to her grave: her father. If you have a wonderful relationship with her, she will always yearn for more time, more love, and more memories. And if you have a painful relationship, she will ache for more healing and closure. Daughters can't escape their fathers. You are linked not by a thread, but by a thick rope, which keeps her need for more of you very strong.

When I interviewed women about their relationships with their dads for *Strong Fathers, Strong Daughters*, they had one of two responses to my questions. They either gushed about your greatness or they burst into tears. That's the power that you have.

Whether you make your daughter breakfast, pack her lunch and drive her to school every day, or you are estranged from her, you need to understand the depth of her desire

> Father!—to God himself we cannot give a holier name.
>
> —*William Wordsworth*

for more of you. She is connected to you by a need-based love, which will stay strong as she matures well into adulthood and, eventually, into her twilight years.

Setting Boundaries

Fathers are their daughters' plumb lines. You establish what is safe and good. You show her how men behave, how they treat women, and whether or not they are trustworthy. To you a spontaneous hug and a kiss may seem to be a small gesture and quite natural for a father to offer his daughter. But from her vantage point, she learns from that act that men are affectionate. They are nice and kind. They won't hurt her. All of your gestures are exaggerated in her mind's eye because you are huge to her. A kiss on the forehead means that she is loved, and she can sleep well that night. When you kiss her again the next day, she learns that men are dependable, and she begins to trust not only you, but she extends that trust to all male figures.

Fathers are the most important men in their daughters' lives for one reason: *you are there first.* Your shaving cream is one of the first male scents that she will know. Your laughter, the depth of your voice, and the feel of your beard make indelible images in her memory and sensibilities. She is stuck with you.

The Pain of Separation

Alicia is forty-five years old. When I first spoke with her about her father, she fought back tears. He was alive and in fact lived very close to her home. But thirty-three years earlier, her parents divorced and she moved out of state with her mother. Her father was so despondent that he simply retreated from her life. For many years, they shared a phone call every few months, and she visited him during the summers. At forty-five years of age, she broke down and sobbed as she remembered the weeks following the divorce. The pain of separation from her father was as fresh thirty-three years later as it was when she was twelve. She adored her father.

Why didn't he come after me? Why did he "allow" my mother to take me so far from him? These were the questions of a twelve-year-old little girl spilling from the mouth of a grown woman. The feelings behind them were raw because during the ensuing thirty-three years, Alicia was stuck on her dad. He disappeared into the background, but her desire for him grew exponentially. Because he didn't realize this (how could he know the heart of his little girl living one thousand miles away?), Alicia's father stayed silent and let her mother rear her, believing that he wasn't needed. He was oblivious to the thick rope that secured her to him.

At seventy years of age, he learned about the rope. Alicia told her father what she longed for as a little girl and her father wept in front of her. He never knew. He couldn't forgive himself. Over time, Alicia helped him see how much she longed for him and the two reconciled. And guess what happened to her relationship with her husband? It became stronger and more peaceful. They fought less.

You are your daughter's plumb line. You establish what is safe and good. You show her how men behave, how they treat women, and whether or not they are trustworthy.

Day Three Challenge: Interview Time

Using a flip video camera or audio recording device, interview your daughter and then reciprocate, allowing her to interview you. Ask silly questions such as, *Would you rather eat a bottle of ketchup or a bottle of mustard?*, as well as serious questions such as, *What's the greatest challenge for you in school?*

When your interviews are complete, upload them to a video sharing site, social media site, or blog.

Checklist

○ Gather needed equipment for your interviews.

○ Make notes about the questions you'd like to ask one another.

○ Choose a time to conduct the interviews. Put it on the calendar!

○ Upload the completed interviews to the Internet.

SECRETS
EVERY
FATHER
SHOULD
KNOW

SECRET 2

She Needs a Hero

Every father leads his daughter somewhere. Ask yourself how and where you are leading your daughter.

What are you doing to lead your daughter in the direction that you want her to go?

Show Her
- How do you model for her courage and tenacity?
- How do you model trustworthiness and honesty?

A New Direction
- Find one way this week where you can actively lead your daughter in a direction she has not gone.
- Does she need to stop acting out?
- Does she need to be bolder with her friends?
- Does she need to act with greater humility, kindness or courage?

Read Chapter Two, "She Needs a Hero," in Strong Fathers, Strong Daughters.

Day Four

Hero Worship—It's Not What You Think

From the moment your daughter first sees you, she gives you hero status. Why? Because every little girl sees her father as larger than life. She wants you to be terrific. So regardless of how terrific you feel, your daughter thinks that you are. You are her hero simply because she wants you to be one. You don't have to earn it; you simply have to maintain your hero status. How do you do that?

Daughters look for different character qualities in heroes than sons do. They want men who live with integrity (you never tell a lie), who will always make them feel safe and protected (even adult women want this), and who are firm but always kind. When you are these things to your daughter, you stay on the hero's platform.

Many of you fathers fail to recognize this. You think that you must be super athletic, extremely smart, or wealthy in order for your children to see you as heroes. This simply isn't true. Some of you believe that your daughters see you as weak or stupid because our culture tells you that your kids see you this way. Nothing could be further from the truth. This is why you may become intimidated when your daughter snarls at you. Her gesture confirms what you think is already true: that she doesn't respect or need you. Don't believe this!

Testing Her Hero

As daughters mature, they test their fathers to see if you can handle them. Sometimes they want to know how patient you are, and if you will lose your temper and topple from the pedestal. So, they push your buttons to see if you are serious about sticking around for the long haul. In short, they run you through the gamut to see if you are really a hero or if you aren't.

When your first grader snubs you, don't take it personally. If your sixth grader challenges your patience by yelling at you that you don't understand her, reprimand her for yelling (in a firm but loving way, letting her know that yelling isn't allowed in your home), and then tell her that you do understand her wishes. The reason this is important is because she needs to know that you are tough enough to handle her. As she matures, she feels a sense of growing independence and will challenge boundaries that you set. Be there to stop her if she wanders too far and reel her back in. Heroes have rules and are clear about them. And heroes always have power to make those rules stick.

> Certain is it that there is no kind of affection so purely angelic as of a father to a daughter. In love to our wives there is desire; to our sons, ambition; but to our daughters there is something, which there are no words to express.
>
> —*Joseph Addison*

Very often fathers fall into the trap of letting their tempers fly either directly to their daughters or in front of them. This is one of the surest ways that you will lose hero status. Dads should always keep their wits about them—not only because your daughter will imitate your behavior; but also because your tone of voice and actions influence how she perceives herself. You always want her perceptions to be strong.

A Lifelong Hero

Tanya's dad was her hero all of her life. As a middle-aged woman, she told me one of the things she admired most about her father was the way he spoke. He was a quiet man, scarce with words; but that fact, she said, made his words carry more punch. "What really impressed me as I got older, was the way he controlled his temper. Growing up, I could tell when he was mad, but I can honestly say that I never heard him yell, swear, or call anyone names. As a teenager, I remember getting rip-roaring mad, and I always remembered my dad and the way he controlled his anger. This made me challenge myself in those angry moments. Many, many times, I held my tongue because I saw my dad do it. Was he my hero? Up until the day he died," she told me. "No one had the integrity and self control like my father had. No one."

I hear stories like these about you fathers all the time. Even adult daughters hold onto heroes. Our husbands usually don't fit the bill because they are contemporaries. They may have the character, but we perceive them as equals, not heroes. That is a position that we understand our daughters will give them and since many of us have had the privilege of having our dads be our heroes, we don't need any more.

Day Four Challenge: Take Your Daughter Dancing

If you are an experienced ballroom dancer, then make a date with your daughter to go dancing. If you need lessons, make a few appointments for the two of you to learn together.

As you learn and practice new steps together, consider how you are leading her and how she is following. Following a real hero is easy because he's honest, trustworthy, and confident. Not only does he have a destination in mind, but he also has a plan about how to reach it.

Use the dance lessons to exercise your heroic qualities. How does leading your daughter in dance equip you for the larger task of leading her in life?

Checklist

O   Schedule dance lessons.

O   Plan the date, place, and time you'll take your daughter dancing.

O   Put it on the calendar!

Day Five

Tag—You're It

Only one generation ago, fathers looked forward to the ultimate compliment: their sons following in their professional footsteps. The tide has changed, and now many fathers enjoy seeing their daughters take on this role. I remember when my own father attended my graduation from medical school. It was the one time I heard him say that he wished that I kept my maiden name after I married. He told me that as I walked across the stage to receive my medical degree, he wanted to hear the professor introduce me as Dr. Jones, not Dr. Meeker. My father graduated from the very same medical school twenty-five years earlier and wanted the audience to identify me as his daughter, not as my husband's wife. I loved that he wanted that.

My dad was proud of me, and I liked that, too. Even now, after he has passed onto Glory, knowing that he was proud of me gives me courage to do things, which I think are impossible. Each time I begin a new book, I feel that I have nothing valuable to write. Then I hear my father's voice. He always told me that I had important things to say. Sure, my husband encourages me, but his words carry a different weight. The reason for this stems from our adult relationship. My father gave me encouragement when I was a child, and his words penetrated my psyche. They changed who I became because his words came at very tender developmental stages in my life.

Watching You Work

Daughters watch their fathers make decisions about their work and then they make decisions too. They watch to see if Dad performs well at his job (financial success isn't important; they look to see if Dad gets compliments on his job) and if his job makes him happy. If they determine that he is good at his job and that it makes him happy, they admire his work and become attracted to it. If a daughter sees that her father is successful and happy in his work, she wants to follow in his footsteps. Daughters want their fathers to feel proud of their work and their accomplishments.

I fear that my generation has become a group of complainers. We criticize fathers for working too much, lamenting that you are never available for your kids. Husbands complain if wives are tired at the end of the day and have nothing leftover to give after spending a day working, taking care of kids, cooking, running errands, and doing chores. We expect too much from one another and this makes our families miserable. Children hear us complain about one another far too frequently. Specifically, I hear women who are stay-at-home mothers complain that their husbands spend too much time at work. Yet they want their husbands to also make more money. Women, we can't have it both ways. If he's home more, he makes less. We get one or the other.

Men do the same. Often husbands want wives who make sure that the kids are emotionally sound, the home is well cared for, and contribute significantly to the household income. Some of us simply can't do this. So fathers and mothers are equally guilty of expecting too much of one another. The real issue is: what do our daughters need in order to become solid, healthy, contributing adults?

Daughters need fathers who work hard. Working at a job that provides for the family is another way to be your daughter's hero. Sure, daughters want more time with their dads, but we also need to understand that those same daughters look up to their fathers and need to see that he is a hard worker. Let's not be fooled: daughters get it when Dad works hard at work. They realize that he is doing something good for them and this makes them feel valuable. Sometimes we mothers need to back off a bit.

Kids boast about their fathers' professions. Consider the girl whose father was a fireman during 9/11. Is her dad her hero? You bet. Think how a sixth grade girl feels when her paramedic father rescues her friend from a bad car accident or how the beloved high school principal's daughter is proud of her father underneath all the inevitable ribbing from her peers.

> If a daughter sees that her father is successful and happy in his work, she wants to follow in his footsteps.

Your work is important to your daughter. Hard work is what heroes do. The money you earn isn't nearly as important to your daughter as the effort you put forth. Maybe you've lost your job. Does that mean that you aren't a hero? Nope. You didn't have control over that. You can be assured, however, that your daughter is watching how you respond to this tough situation. Will you complain about the lack of fairness in life, or will you press forward to find a new job?

Day Five Challenge: Take Your Daughter to Work

The "Take Our Daughters and Sons to Work Day" event is generally held in the spring each year. You can find more information about this online at www.daughtersandsonsnetwork.org. Plan to bring your daughter to your workplace on this special day (once you have received approval from your manager and her school). Before the day, set aside a few tasks, if possible, that she can help you complete or that she can do on her own. Involve her as much as possible in the "normal" office routine, including attending staff meetings and lunch appointments.

If you are not able to bring your daughter into your workplace, consider how you can still invite her to work alongside you. Teach her how to do certain chores that you usually do (whether it's mowing the grass or buying the week's groceries). Talk to her about how important it is to work hard at these basic tasks that keep the home running smoothly.

How you approach your work—whether at the office or at home—matters to your daughter. Today examine your attitude about it. Do you complain about your job?

Make a point to communicate a positive attitude about your work this week. Tell your daughter that you are grateful that you have a job because hard work is a blessing.

Heroes like hard work.

Checklist

O Get approval from your manager and her school to bring your daughter to work.

O Choose a date and time to bring your daughter to work or have her work with you at home.

O Plan tasks for your daughter to do and meetings for her to attend with you at your workplace. At home, give her specific chores to complete.

O Put it on the calendar!

Day Six

Lead Like No One Else

A peculiar dynamic has taken hold in parenting in the 21st century. Children, rather than parents, have become the leaders in the homes.

If a child wants a cell phone, she gets one, even if her parents believe that she shouldn't have one. If a daughter wants to play three extracurricular sports, she plays them, even if it means having her parents surrender weekend family time. We have become consumed with pleasing our children to the point where even they don't know what they want anymore. We have come by this honestly. We read parenting books in order to understand our children's needs. We scour psychology articles in order to get a handle on our children's feelings so that we will not harm them. While learned knowledge can be helpful, it should never be substituted for intuition.

> If you want your daughter to grow up to be a strong leader one day, you must be bold as one now.

Looking to You for Leadership

Every daughter looks to her father for leadership. Your daughter sees you as the one who is smarter and more experienced, and even though her body language may make you feel otherwise, she respects your advice. When she is a toddler, she looks to you to show her where she should walk and where she shouldn't. She may even touch something that she knows is dangerous simply to see if you are watching. And when she grows older, she wants to know what you think she should study, what sports she should try, or which musical instrument she might play. In short, she wants you to lead her in all areas of her life. The reason is simple; she doesn't know what you know about life.

Girls who lead their parents are miserably unhappy. When a daughter's whims and wishes determine a family's vacations, choice of schools, mealtimes, and weekend plans, the entire family is miserable. Life isn't meant to be lived this way. She knows that when she is born, she is to meld into the family; the family isn't to orbit her. Sadly, many fathers fear stepping into a leadership role in the family because they believe that everyone will be unhappy. Nothing could be further from the truth.

Every father has an instinct to lead his family—particularly his daughter. You know what you want for her. You know what is best for her, so *act on that*. Don't be bashful—even if everyone around you tells you that your job is to take a backseat. Your job as the only father to your daughter is to be a strong leader. Every strong and effective leader produces strong and effective leaders. If you want your daughter to grow up to be a strong leader one day, you must be bold as one now.

Your daughter looks to you to lead her like no one else will. Remember, as the one assigned to the hero's platform, you have a position to uphold. You are connected to her in a way that no one else is; you are connected to her by her need and love for you. Her mother is connected similarly, but she's not on the platform. She may be one day, but you are already there. So use that platform to launch your daughter to a great place.

How Do You Lead?

First, listen to your intuition. If your heart tells you that she can do better in school, then challenge her. If it tells you that she should try a new sport, encourage her. If you feel that she is over-scheduled and not getting enough time with you or the family, then insist that she drop an activity. Good leaders make hard decisions. And no one in the family will make those decisions unless you do. Many fathers hesitate leading because they fear that their daughters will become alienated from them; don't be afraid. Daughters who get into trouble aren't daughters who are led properly; they are girls who never bump up against strong leadership.

Think about the heroes in your own life. Are they weak? Indecisive? Lackadaisical?

Of course not. They think clearly, make tough decisions, and step out in front of those whom they want to influence. That's what your daughter wants you to do with her. Walk ahead of her and lead.

Day Six Challenge: Lead Your Daughter to Hidden Treasure

Go Geocaching with your daughter. Geocaching is easy and fun. First, find directional coordinates for hidden treasures online, and then use a GPS device or smartphone to find the caches. Sign the log when you find the treasure. (More complete instructions are online at the Geocaching website at www.geocaching.com.)

As you seek the hidden treasure, pay close attention to how you lead the hunt and how your daughter follows.

Checklist

O Choose a day and time to go Geocaching.

O Put it on the calendar!

O The day of the hunt: Online, find four or five caches and print directions and/or send them to your smartphone.

O Make sure you have a full tank of gas, hop in the car, and hunt!

SECRETS
EVERY
FATHER
SHOULD
KNOW

SECRET 3

You Are Her First Love

Your daughter's experience with loving and being loved begins with you. You're there first for her. Every man who enters her life will be compared to you. Her opinions about loving relationships are being formed now.

- Do you think your daughter knows—really knows—that you love her? Why or why not?
- What are some ways that you demonstrate your love to your daughter?
- What are some things you could do differently in order to better communicate your love to your daughter?

Read Chapter Three, "You Are Her First Love," in Strong Fathers, Strong Daughters.

Day Seven

Love—the Dos and Don'ts

Men love differently than women. That's why you scratch your head in confusion when your daughter or wife cries and insists that you just don't understand. They want you to know what they want, like, and need without ever telling you. You, on the other hand, love deeply but differently.

Attention and Adoration

As you work on your relationship with your daughter, you must remember that different things will make her feel loved than what make you feel loved. First, she feels loved when you pay attention to her. When she comes home from a soccer game and you ask if she wants to go have ice cream because you want to hear all about her game, she feels loved. When she goes on a date and comes home at midnight, she feels loved if you are up waiting for her. Sure, you can ask how her time was, but the mere fact that you cared enough to make sure she got home safely makes her feel deeply loved.

Women, like men, want to feel that someone in their lives adores them. Adoration is different from respecting or admiring another. Adoration is the sense that you can do no wrong. Why should you communicate this to your daughter when she, of course, makes mistakes? Because she needs it from you. Your daughter has a space in her heart designated for you alone. No one else can occupy that spot.

When you express your adoration to her, she realizes that you have a spot in your heart just for her. A father who adores his daughter holds her in high esteem, wants only the best for her, and feels that no one in the world compares with her. She is more beautiful, kinder, and stronger than all women (or girls) her age. Every daughter wants her father to feel this way about her. And she wants her father to express this to her.

> A father is always making his baby into a little woman. And when she is a woman he turns her back again.
>
> —*Enid Bagnold*

Our culture ties girls in knots, and your daughter is no exception. No matter how hard you try to isolate her from the ugly influences of a world that sexualizes and degrades women, you can't. And since you are the primary means by which she develops a healthy sense of beauty and sexuality, when it comes to shaping these in her, it's on your shoulders. When it comes to loving your daughter, remember these important ideas:

- **Do tell her that you love her.** Tell her as frequently as feels natural to you. Sometimes you may feel timid, but press through the discomfort. Every daughter needs to hear *I love you* from her dad.
- **Do express adoration.** Let her know that she is the apple of your eye. If you have multiple daughters, tell each one of them at different times.
- **Do believe in her.** If the two of you don't get along well and fight constantly, you can still show her that you believe in her.

Examine her character and find what is good in her. Look deeply into her life and find her natural gifts. Then, communicate to her that you are her "number one fan." Tell her that you know that she can succeed. You know that she is smarter than she thinks, wiser than she believes, and far more capable than she realizes. Communicating this is extremely important because most girls, particularly during the teen years, feel terribly inadequate, dumb, and unattractive. You need to really amp up your positive comments during the tough times and help her combat those feelings.

- **Don't remark on her weight—EVER.** No pet names for parts of her body, no calling her "sexy," and no telling her that she's chubby or that she should lose a few pounds. No matter what you say about her weight, she will hear in her mind, *My dad thinks I'm fat; therefore, I'm ugly.* Since you can't win, avoid this. I can't tell you the number of messes that I've been involved in undoing with daughters whose fathers have innocently commented about their weight as they are growing up.

- **Don't remark on her looks very often.** I know that this feels counterintuitive. Shouldn't every girl know that her dad thinks she's beautiful? Of course; but don't overdo it. You don't want her to feel that her appearance is a priority to you. Remember, when you comment on something, it lets the hearer know that the topic is significant to you (otherwise, why would you comment on it?). You want to be sure that your daughter knows that what you really cherish about her is her inner beauty. So talk about that.

- **Don't spare words of encouragement and affection.** Girls use more words, and they bond through words. Girls feel that words connect them with others. So tell your daughter what you admire about her and tell her why. I promise that if you are sincere, your words will change the woman that she becomes.

Day Seven Challenge: Go Shopping

This may be quite a stretch for you, Dad, but chances are, your daughter loves shopping. This outing doesn't have to be an expensive one (set rules about spending before you leave). Devote one day doing what she enjoys at the mall. Eat lunch in the food court and check out the specials at the makeup counter. Really pay attention to what excites her and defines her style. She'll feel adored when you do.

Checklist

O Choose a day to spend with your daughter at the mall.

O Put it on the calendar!

O Decide on your budget for the day and stick to it.

Day Eight

Words—Use Them

You know that your daughter talks more than you do. Maybe this confounds you or irritates you. Regardless, that's the way she's wired, and it's wonderful for her that you aren't wired the same. The very fact that she talks more than you do gives you an opportunity to listen to her better than those who use as many words as she does. You don't compete for verbal space like her friends and mother do. You are a good listener because you don't feel a constant urge to interrupt, interject, or speak over her. That makes *you* the perfect listener in her eyes.

There are times, however, that she does need to hear from you. Just as you can't read her inner thoughts and feelings, she can't read yours. And while you don't need to be overly verbose, she needs to know a few of your key ideas and feelings. The only way to assure that she knows them is for you to articulate them in a loving way and at times when she will really listen. So what are these things that she needs to hear?

She Needs to Hear From You

First, she needs to hear, "I love you." Many fathers assume that their daughters intuitively know that they love them. Let me tell you that they don't. There is a secret that fathers need to know when it comes to love and your daughters. As far as daughters are concerned, their mother's love is non-negotiable. Yours, on the other hand, is negotiable (in her mind). Regardless of how you feel, this is how many daughters perceive their father's love. Daughters feel that they must be careful to earn their father's love. They don't assume that it is there. Mom, they believe, will never go anywhere. You, on the other hand, might. Again, this is completely independent of what you feel or communicate. It just is. So you need to go the extra mile or two to communicate to your daughter that no matter what, you will always love her. She needs to know deep in her soul that, even if she sat in a closet for an entire year, you would love her the same as if she got straight A's in school.

Second, daughters need to know *why* you love them. I know this sounds a bit over the top, but daughters don't always settle for, "I love you because I'm your dad." They want to know what it is about them that you like. What do you see in her that she can't see herself that gives her value?

When you tell her that you love her, always be ready for the follow up question, "Why, Dad?" Have the answers ready and be as concrete as possible with them. For instance, if you love her because there is no one else on the earth just like her, tell her. Perhaps you love her because you prayed for a daughter for many years before she was born, or because she has your smile. Find something very unique and honest and then let her know what that special thing about her is that helps you love her so much.

Third, she needs to hear what your hopes for her are. Don't hold back here and don't leave her wondering what you want for her. It's very important for a daughter to know that her father believes that she has a good future and more—that she is capable of living up to high moral, ethical, and academic standards. Girls whose fathers communicate reasonable but high expectations grow up believing that they can make good decisions and that they can live against the grain of a society that tells them that their worth lies in their sexuality or in their physical beauty.

Finally, using words helps you bond with her. Men and boys bond through physical activity; girls and women bond through conversation. While this may not feel natural to you, try to engage her in conversation as naturally as possible. Ask her questions about her friends—not in a derogatory or judgmental way—but from a genuine desire to want to know them better. Ask her what she thinks about politics or books—even ask her advice about your work. If your daughter feels that you value her input, she will not only feel closer to you, but she'll also feel more confident in her ability to make good decisions.

Girls whose fathers communicate reasonable but high expectations grow up believing that they can make good decisions and that they can live against the grain of a society that tells them that their worth lies in their sexuality or in their physical beauty.

Day Eight Challenge: Take Your Daughter on a Date

This week, plan a special time for you and your daughter to go on a date together. You may choose to take her out for a nice dinner, for a picnic in the park, or to see your favorite sports team play ball.

During this time, plan to say, "I love you" when you know that she'll really hear it. Even if she doesn't ask you why you love her, tell her anyway (this requires some forethought, so think ahead).

What do you love about her? How are you going to articulate that?

Checklist

○ Plan a special time for your date. Whether you choose a fancy restaurant and you dress in your best or you opt for hot dogs and nachos at a hockey game, pay attention to the details of the date. Clear all distractions. Both of you should turn off your cell phones, focusing on your time together.

○ Put it on the calendar!

No Middle Ground

When it comes to loving fathers, for most daughters, there is no middle ground. That's because daughters feel very intense feelings toward their dads. When they hurt, the pain they carry stays very deep. And when they have a good relationship with their fathers, the joy they feel is magnified. That's the intensity of the feelings that daughters have toward their fathers. It is a mystery like no other.

Dad Gives Something Different

When your daughter first sees you, she knows that you are not her mother. You are different. Your voice is deeper and more frightening and somehow more comforting. Your face is not smooth like her mother's, and she knows that you care for her differently. Not better or worse, just differently from her mother. I have watched newborn daughters cry in their mothers' arms and refuse to stop. Then, when their father holds them, they quiet. Little girls know that Dad has something different to offer than Mom does. He doesn't have breast milk or a soft voice, but he brings security, which feels very good to a child rendered completely dependent on the love of another to keep her alive.

From the very beginning, a daughter learns that when her father comforts her, she is safe; when her father holds her, she won't fall and when her father smothers her with kisses, she has a love that will last for a lifetime. Her knowledge is intuitive. And it stays with her for the rest of her life. I don't know why, but a daughter feels that her mother's love is different. It isn't more fragile, but it feels less intense. Perhaps it's fear or respect for a father that she doesn't always feel toward her mother. Perhaps she is taught that her mother can't leave, but her father can. That's why she hangs on to every touch, tone of voice, or inflection emanating from her father's mouth. She feels a sense of power in her father's love that she doesn't feel anywhere else in the world. What Dad says matters. What he thinks is important. And what he believes about her shapes the way she thinks about herself.

> Every daughter wants a little more of her dad every day of her life.

This is tough stuff to hear, but every father needs to hear it because one day someone will ask your daughter a question about you. When they do, will she burst into tears because of the painful history between the two of you, or will she gush about how wonderful you are? Now is the time to ask the questions.

Every daughter is born with a father-shaped hole in her heart. Even girls who are raised by single mothers and who have never met their fathers have an internal ache to find them. They want to know one thing: *Why didn't you stay?* I have spoken with girls whose fathers never even saw them, and they have cried as young women wondering what was wrong with them that caused their father to walk away from them. Of course an adult father would say that his leaving had nothing to do with his daughter. Many divorced fathers say this. They know that for very personal and private reasons, they chose not to stay with their daughter's mother. But this is the thinking of an adult man, not that of a small daughter. She believes that something was wrong with her. Even when she is grown, she will feel broken and unworthy of her father's love. Her feelings will be that of a wounded little girl, not of a grown woman, because her hurt started as a child and never matured out of that.

Wanting More of Dad

Even grown women long for their fathers. Every daughter, regardless of her age, wants more of her father. She wants more love and more time, or she wants more healing. The hole in the heart stays empty until Dad occupies the space. When she has a healthy relationship with him, the hole is filled to overflowing. When she has lost her father or has never had a good relationship, the hole feels only partially filled.

What your daughter feels in her own heart is in your hands. The question for every father is: *Are you willing to do whatever it takes to ensure that your daughter doesn't live her life feeling empty because the two of you have had a rift?* Perhaps you have had a fight that was never resolved. You need to know that it is never too late as far as your daughter is concerned. Never. Every daughter wants a little more of her dad every day of her life.

Day Nine Challenge: Write Your Daughter a Letter

Understanding that your daughter has a hole in her heart with your name on it, ask yourself, "How much of that is occupied by me?" Does she feel a void because you haven't gotten along? Does she feel empty because you haven't been involved in her life as much as you should have been?

Today, write her a letter. Tell her what you feel toward her and if there are hurts that need healing, ask for her forgiveness. Make that first step toward building a better relationship.

Even if you have a solid relationship with your daughter, write her a letter. Tell her what she means to you.

Checklist

O Find a quiet hour or two in your schedule so that you can really pour out your heart to your daughter.

O Put it on the calendar!

O Go to the library, a coffee shop, or close the door to your home office while you write. Turn off your cell phone and laptop.

O Even if you have lousy penmanship, try to write neatly and don't print a computer-generated letter. Your daughter will cherish having this letter in your own handwriting in ink on paper.

O Seal it and surprise your daughter with the letter. Put it in her backpack, under her pillow, or send it to her home.

Teach Her Humility

This secret requires a personal buy-in on your part, which will probably dictate some serious soul searching.

Do *you* possess true humility?

Regarding Others
- Write down a few adjectives about how you feel about the value of your spouse, your friends, and your coworkers. Do you perceive yourself as better than they are, or do you feel that you are of equal value?

A Critical Spirit
- Do you constantly criticize friends, family members, and coworkers?
- Write down the handful of people that you criticize. Why do you look down on them?
- Then, make a point of speaking to those people this week and deliberately change the way you talk to them. And if possible, make the changes in front of your daughter.

Read Chapter Four, "Teach Her Humility," in Strong Fathers, Strong Daughters.

Day Ten

The Firm Foundation

When it comes to your daughter, you are the brick and mortar guy. You lay the foundation of all good things in her life. She learns the big lessons in life from you. That's why it is very important that you be the one to teach her about her real value and the value of other people. So when it comes to teaching her virtues like humility, you're the one assigned the job.

Reclaiming and Reassessing Humility

As I discuss in *Strong Fathers, Strong Daughters*, humility is a forgotten virtue. This is due primarily to the fact that we live in a culture, which tells parents that they should bolster their child's self-esteem any way possible. We should clap for their successes, no matter how large, small, real, or imagined. Of course, building self-esteem is important, but life should never be centered completely around oneself. This leads to misery. And I see many parents do this to their children. You don't want to be a dad who does this.

Furthermore, humility has also been grossly misunderstood. It is not about self-deprecation—quite the opposite. It is about instilling a deep sense of respect and love for oneself in a child. A daughter who is humble knows that she doesn't need to look farther than her own family to realize that she has extraordinary worth. And when a girl feels good about who she is, she is able to feel less threatened by her peers. She can embrace them as having value, talents, and gifts that she doesn't have. She doesn't feel threatened by others' successes because she feels so good about who she is.

But humility takes her deeper than that. Living with humility allows your daughter to know that others around her are no better and no worse than she is. She neither elevates herself above them nor does she look down on others. You don't want her to do these things, because when she does, she separates herself from other girls and becomes disconnected from them. Then, she will live in her own protected, walled-off world. And this is a very lonely place to be.

You know girls who do this. They pretend to be better than others. They exude an air of superiority. We adults know that this is all a show and that it reveals a deep-seated insecurity. The sad part is that girls who do this put themselves at arm's distance from their friends, and they end up very lonely. Daughters with humility rarely end up lonely because they understand that with all people, they have a connection. They, like others, are humans with great value, regardless of their accomplishments. They and the people they engage are valuable simply because they are alive.

Modeling Humility

So what can you do to instill humility in your daughter? Here's where the going gets a bit trickier. You model it. And you can only model it if first you do some real soul searching. Think about how you really feel about others. Are you a snob? Do you perceive yourself to be better than other men, smarter than others, or wealthier than others and, therefore, more valuable than they?

Or do you see others as having the exact same worth that you do? Men who believe this are delightful to be around. They are not easily intimidated or threatened, and they are never defensive.

One of the best ways to model humility to your daughter is to work alongside her. Take her to work with you and let her see how you treat your coworkers and your boss. When you leave their presence, don't talk negatively about them behind their backs; rather, talk positively about them and show her that you value the work they do and the people that they are. Speak as positively about the woman cleaning your office as the client whose business you are trying to secure.

A daughter listens to the tone of her father's voice when he speaks, so make sure that your daughter hears you compliment —not criticize—others. This will give her a very clear sense that you perceive them to be as valuable as everyone else, including yourself.

My father didn't tell me how to live;
he lived, and let me watch him do it.
—Clarence B. Kelland

Day Ten Challenge: Connect Her to the Past

There's something about knowing your roots to solidify your identity and self-worth. A daughter who understands the strength of her foundation is better equipped to stand firm.

Find a way to connect your daughter with her "ancient history." Together, you could begin researching your family history and create a detailed scrapbook for future generations to enjoy. Or you may choose to simply visit an elderly relative and talk for a while about what he or she remembers about childhood, holidays, and other family memories.

Another idea is to watch your wedding video with your daughter then flip through the wedding photo album. Talk about how much you and her mother were in love and tell her funny stories about the day. Do the same with her birth video and/or baby book.

Checklist

○ Plan which family history activity you'd like to do with your daughter.

○ Arrange to visit relatives who can meet with you.

○ If you are planning to research your family history together, be prepared to allot several different research sessions, depending on where the information takes you.

○ Put it on the calendar!

○ If you're watching videos together, make it a "movie night" with popcorn and soda.

Day Eleven

Give Her a Story

Your daughter will become a very unique woman because she will have watched you for many years. When she hears you speak kindly, she will imitate your inflections to see if speaking kindly works for her. If you yell, she will yell at someone. If you behave in a way that demonstrates that you respect others, she will mimic your behavior primarily because she admires you but also to test your behaviors to see how effective they are for her. She wants to know if speaking the way you do and treating others as you do makes her feel good about life.

She's Watching You

When it comes to teaching your daughter the significant lessons in life, your behavior stands out as the major influence. That's why you must be your own toughest critic when it comes to your behavior. She is watching every movement, every sneeze, and every argument. In a very real sense, your story can become her story. How many fathers in sales watch their daughters grow up to be saleswomen? How many physician fathers have physician daughters? Look around you. Sons aren't the only ones who grow up to follow in their father's footsteps. Daughters do the same.

Your daughter needs to learn about humility for reasons we have explained earlier. As you read the chapter on humility in *Strong Fathers, Strong Daughters*, get tough on yourself and ask some hard questions like, "Do I live with a sense that others have equal value to me or do I believe in my heart that I am better than others?" What you find out about your feelings is extremely important because your daughter will pick up on your exact feelings. She is sharp and in tune with you. Keep pushing yourself and figure out what you really think about humility. Have you misunderstood it? Do you think that humility is for wimps or strong men? Be brutally honest with yourself because her future may rest to some degree on how you feel about others and yourself. In other words, if you look down on friends, your wife, or your colleagues, she will grow up to do the same. And the problem for her, if she looks down on others, is that she will be a very lonely person. You may survive loneliness, but she won't fare as well with it. She may be a more social being.

> A daughter who is humble knows that she doesn't need to look farther than her own family to realize that she has extraordinary worth.

One of the cruelest things that parents teach their daughters is a sense of superiority or entitlement. I see this all the time. Many parents are well-meaning, hoping to teach their daughters that they are smart, strong, independent thinkers, but they take an ugly turn along the way. Rather than instill confidence in girls, they teach them that they are better than their peers. Rather than encourage them to be thoughtful, parents imbue daughters with a sense of self-centeredness, which turns off friends, peers, and coworkers. Don't do this to your daughter. Make sure that before she leaves home, she has a deep sense of her own worth, and that she values all people—those whom she loves and those whom she doesn't. And most importantly, make sure that you are the one who teaches her these things through modeling humility.

So give her a story. Act in a way that provides opportunities for you to show her what humility looks like, talks like, and feels like. Get around people who bring this out in you. How? Find ways to serve other human beings.

Serve Others

If you aren't a help to your spouse around the house, get moving. Do the dishes; help out with the laundry. If you are already a star in those areas, move beyond the confines of your family to find ways to serve other humans. Get involved in a soup kitchen or a food drive. Show her a different way to live than she gets to see anywhere else.

When our girls were young, I ordered Chinese takeout for dinner and asked my husband to pick it up. Just before my husband left the house, I reminded him to be sure that egg rolls were included in our order because they were my favorite part of the meal. Two of our daughters jumped in the car with him to pick up the food.

When he returned home, I became agitated because the egg rolls weren't in the white containers. When I let my irritation show (I barked at him) about forgetting the egg rolls, he stayed silent. My six-year-old tugged on my sleeve and whispered that her father spotted a man rummaging through garbage cans on their way home from the restaurant. He pulled his car into the parking lot near the garbage can and brought our entire order of food over to the man. He then told the gentleman that he was welcome to any or all of the food. You guessed it. He took my egg rolls.

Our daughters learned to treat others as they would like to be treated because my husband gave them a story. It was his story born from a strong belief that all people deserve to be loved at all times.

Day Eleven Challenge: Serve Together

Find a need among your friends, family members, or neighbors and ask your daughter to help you meet it. Ask her to help you put up dry wall at a friend's home, mow the lawn for an elderly neighbor, or repair the car of someone on a fixed income for free. You get the idea. Be creative with ways to help others out and then ask her to join you in doing so.

You may also choose to work together for a local charity or church project and/or help out in a recurring voluntary role. Encourage your daughter to see the needs around her and cheerfully volunteer her time and energy to serve others.

Checklist

○ Find a need and/or a charity or church project in which you could assist.

○ Plan the date and time to serve together.

○ Put it on the calendar!

○ Wear old work clothes, pack your lunch and water bottle, and get to work.

Extend an Invitation

One of the toughest aspects of parenting is to get kids to do what you really want them to do. Fathers prod, cajole, argue, and demand. I have seen fathers bribe their daughters to get good grades, threaten daughters with being grounded if they don't meet curfew, and even pay them for being nice. Sometimes we feel desperate to do whatever is necessary to get our kids to behave.

As a father, you want your daughter to shine. You want her to be respectful, intelligent, and delightful. This is natural and your desire to do whatever you can to help her succeed is not only admirable, but it also means that you are acting on wonderful, fatherly instincts. The very fact that you are so heavily invested emotionally, physically, and mentally in her welfare means that you are a really good dad. The only trouble that you have is getting her to do what you really want her to do. "How," you wonder, "will I get her to listen to my sage advice?"

Tip the Scales

There are ways that you can do this. In fact, there are secrets that many influential fathers know. One is to tip the scales. Here's where most good fathers get off track: they work to balance discipline and fun, and this doesn't work. You need to always tip the scales in a positive direction. One act of discipline to one act of levity never works. Daughters are far too sensitive for this. Whenever you discipline, you must offset the episode with at least four episodes of fun and positive interaction. Discipline always feels hurtful and leaves a bad taste in a daughter's mouth, and if you want her listening to you again and enjoying your company, you must tip the scales toward positive interaction.

Very often I hear fathers complain that their daughters won't listen to them. They insist that their daughters don't respect them and that most of their interactions with their daughters are unpleasant. This is particularly true during the teen years when fathers recognize that the stakes are higher. When a daughter makes a mistake, the consequences are far more serious. So, most dads really intensify efforts at discipline. This is excellent. The only thing these great dads forget is that they also need to intensify efforts at offsetting the negative times. They need to reach out to their daughters to spend times together that are pleasant—not stressful.

> One act of discipline to one act of levity never works. Daughters are far too sensitive for this. Whenever you discipline, you must off-set the episode with at least four episodes of fun and positive interaction.

Even if daughters rebuff you, ask again and again, letting them know that regardless of negativity surrounding discipline, you still want their company.

When it comes to influencing your daughter to treat others well and to respect herself, you need to win. If your daughter leaves home without a clear sense of her own worth or without a healthy perspective regarding how to treat others, she is in for a miserable life.

As you have read, teaching her humility is the best way to shift her perspective regarding who she is and how valuable others are. You can tell her how valuable she is. And this is important. You can discuss the importance of treating others well and correct her when she fails to do so. This is also important. But what will really teach her these valuable lessons is to invite her to work alongside you while you serve.

Invite Her Help

Show her how to work as a team. I guarantee that when she serves beside you, you will have to use very few words when it comes to teaching her about her own value and the value of others. And there is an extraordinary added benefit here. As you work with her, the two of you will have fun. You will not only be teaching her great life lessons, but you will also have fun together, thereby helping you tip the scales when it comes to spending more positive time together.

Many fathers erroneously feel that when their daughters hit the teen years, Dad's influence dries up. I can tell you that the very opposite is true. The teen years are the time when daughters look more intently to their fathers for direction and influence. These are the years that you need to really pour it on. The good news is that, although your daughter will act as if she doesn't want an invitation from you, deep down, she is craving one. So give it to her.

Day Twelve Challenge: Spa or Dress-Up Time

Here's a fun way to "tip the scales." Spend some time in your daughter's world of make-believe and dress-up. Help her transform into her favorite princess or super-hero by putting on costumes and makeup. If you are good at face painting, give her cheeks some colorful pictures or design her face into a favorite animal.

If your daughter is older, simply give her a spa gift basket with some bubble bath and candles. Create a quiet space for her to unwind after a tough sports practice or a hard exam. Once she's in her pajamas, tuck her in bed and invite her to tell you about her day.

Checklist

○ For a make-believe time, gather play makeup, costumes, face paints, and dress-up items.

○ Decide on a day when the two of you can play together, uninterrupted. Put it on the calendar!

○ To give your daughter a spa gift basket, purchase a bottle of bubble bath and a small votive candle in a glass holder at a drugstore or supermarket. Put the items into a small basket.

○ Have the basket ready following her next big exam (or another important event). Put it on the calendar!

SECRETS
EVERY
FATHER
SHOULD
KNOW

SECRET 5

Protect Her, Defend Her
(and use a shotgun, if necessary)

Popular culture trains our daughters for a life of promiscuity. If you don't want your daughter to be sexually active in high school, you need to tell her and teach her. You, Dad, are your daughter's most effective protector and defender against a world that's set against her.

Building Character
- Write down four character qualities that you want your daughter to have when she's twenty-five:

- Now identify what influences she faces that will work against the development of those character qualities:

Make a plan to limit their influence. Limit her television time, the kind of music that she listens to, and the movies that she watches.

Teaching Sexuality
- Reread Chapter One in *Strong Fathers, Strong Daughters*. Make a timeline of your daughter's life beginning with her current age. Write down what you want her to know at each age about her sexuality.
- If she is in middle school or junior high, find out what sex ed program her school uses and look at it. Then set aside a time to talk to her about it.
- If she is in high school, set aside a time to talk about dating. And most importantly, make your own rules for her dating and communicate those to her.

Read Chapter Five, "Protect Her, Defend Her (and use a shotgun if necessary)" in Strong Fathers, Strong Daughters.

Day Thirteen

The World's Tough,
But Not As Tough As You Are

If I had to pinpoint one problem that trips fathers up more than anything else, it would be fear. From the time a daughter is born, a father feels a strong sense of inadequacy in being able to successfully protect his daughter. As she grows older, her world becomes larger, and the influences outside of your domain become more intense. Even when she is in second grade, you feel that you are losing her because her teacher now has influence, television has influence, and of course, dangers lurk around every corner that you simply can't anticipate or prevent.

The truth is, the world is a tough place for a young, tender girl. That's why God gives a daughter a father. And I am a firm believer that if you were inadequate for the job, you would have never been assigned it. It's certainly a job that isn't for wimps, but you are wired with everything that you need to do a really good job. I am also convinced that fathers should never parent out of fear but out of strength. Yes, there are influences beyond you and dangers that you can't prevent for your daughter, but many, many more exist that are preventable. If you focus on those and let God take care of the rest, you can have a wonderful life with your daughter.

Instilling Character in Her

Regardless of her age at this moment, think of the major character qualities that you want to instill in your daughter. Do you want her to be strong, independent, kind, courageous, astute, and humble? Do you want her to love with a sense of pride and healthy modesty about her body and her intellectual abilities? Ponder these things. When she is twenty-five, what kind of woman do you hope that she will be? A word of caution is necessary. I'm not referring to her achievements and certainly not her appearance; these are things that the culture around her pressures her to focus on. I'm referring to her character.

This is a very important exercise because every father teaches his daughter many things about herself, wittingly or unwittingly. The lessons are too important and your influence in her character development is much too great to ignore. If you make a simple list of character qualities that you want to see her develop, then you will purposefully help her become those things. You will become her advocate and her partner. She will see you as one who has linked arms with her as she walks through life, not one who opposes her at every turn. This is extremely important because most girls grow up with the sense that they and the culture around them are a team and Dad is the enemy. He is on "the other side" if you will, the one who never understands. This is a subtle alliance but one that is important to recognize; every girl needs to know that her dad is always on her side, and the culture around her is the enemy. The sad truth is, most girls that I see don't see

> Every girl needs to know that her dad is always on her side, and the culture around her is the enemy.

things this way. They genuinely believe that songwriters, magazine editors, and even physicians and health care providers who work in teen clinics are stronger advocates for her than her own dad. Don't ever let her believe this.

So make a plan. Determine to let her know that you and she are a team. No, you are not equal partners or friends; you are a father-daughter team and you, as her father, will always have her back. Always. You, like no one else, understand her and advocate for her because the two of you are linked with an intense familial love. No one else out there loves her the way you do. She needs to know this. The great thing is, you can communicate this to her when she is three, thirteen, thirty, and even sixty. You and she will always be a team.

Make a list of the lessons that her culture tries to teach her. Look around in her world and try to see what she sees. What does pop music tell her? What are friends influencing her to do? What do boys want from her? What are clothing companies teaching her about where her value comes from? These are the enemy camps. Yes, they have influence, but since you are the one who is really on her team and the two of you are connected with deeper bonds than these camps will ever have in her life, you and she will win. When it comes to helping her develop into a strong young woman, you are tougher than all of these camps rolled into one.

Day Thirteen Challenge: Do an Art Project Together

Work as a team to create an art project. It could be a simple snowflake cut from folded paper, or you could choose to do something more involved, particularly if one of you is artistic. Some other ideas: use crayons, watercolors, finger paints, or modeling clay for an at-home project. Visit a paint-your-own pottery store to create a decorated item to take home.

Checklist

O   Choose a time to work together on an art project.

O   Put it on the calendar!

O   Gather or purchase needed supplies.

O   Check pottery store hours and cost, if you choose that option.

No Back Seat Boys

When you were in high school, you had many thoughts and feelings about sex. Since you are a visual person, images of sexy women triggered feelings that were very intense. As an adult now, you can look back on those years through a different lens and understand the struggles with which teen boys contend.

What you need to realize is that your teenage daughter doesn't experience life the same way that you did as a teenage boy. She sees those same glossy images of sexy women, and different feelings are triggered in her. She feels that she should be sexy, thin, and attractive to boys her age. You saw the images and wanted sex, perhaps; she sees those images and wants to change who she is. The more she sees, the more convinced she becomes that she isn't good enough as she already is. If she's to be popular, highly regarded, or cool, she must be, above all, sexier.

But this isn't her only problem. She truly doesn't understand that when a boy sees her in a skimpy shirt, he gets as turned on as he does. She thinks she's pretty and attractive. She wants him to look at her and think that she's mature and lovely. She doesn't want him to look at her lustfully; she wants him to think that she's pretty.

And one more thing: her mother understands that boys look at her differently, but even she doesn't understand to the extent that you do because you were once a teen boy. She wasn't.

You Know How Boys Think

That's why your daughter needs you to stand in the gap. You get boys. You know what they will think and feel if she walks into school wearing a tight, skimpy top or a skirt that barely covers her rear end. And you, most certainly, do not want any boy looking at her that way. You want him to respect and revere her, not look at her as an easy roll in the back seat of his beat up Taurus.

Here's an important secret that you must know about teenage girls and sex. They don't want sex for sexual satisfaction because most don't really get it with teenage boys. Girls want sex for male attention and affection. Period. They want boys to have sex with them so that they will feel cared for and adored. But you know that teen boys are not usually concerned with a girl's feelings. After having sex with their boyfriends (or even boys that they've hooked up with), scores of teen girls have sat in my office in tears because they didn't feel adored, respected, or loved. In fact, most got just the opposite from the boys with whom they had had sex; they eventually got dumped.

Determine that this is not going to happen to your precious daughter. How do you do that? It isn't rocket science, and it's easier than you think. Give her attention. Make sure that you are affectionate with her. That's it. Give these two things to her repeatedly and consistently, and you have just wielded the fiercest weapon that you can against her ending up in the backseat of some pimple-faced fellow's car. You win.

But you may be saying to yourself, "Great idea, but my teenage daughter won't let me within ten feet of her. Show her affection? Not going to happen." Many fathers feel this way because girls naturally pull away from their fathers when they hit puberty. They become uncomfortable with you as a man and with themselves as young women. They don't want to be treated like little girls any-more, and they want to feel that they can make their own decisions without parental help. But you know better. You felt a bit this way as a young teen boy when your own mother tried to hug you or tell you what to do.

So give her slack and space. Change the way you show her affection, but never back off completely. She needs you more than she knows, so realize this truth for her. If she doesn't want you to touch her in public, don't. Do it privately. If she doesn't want a full frontal hug, touch her shoulders or the top of her head. Some girls are shier than others. If your daughter is shy, then approach her cautiously. When she gets into bed at night, go into her room and give her a peck on the cheek. Pull the covers over her shoulders and ask if she needs another blanket. Then sit on the edge of her bed and ask how her day was. No matter how long it takes, keep your attention and affection in forward motion.

> Give your daughter attention and affection repeatedly and con-sistently, and you have just wielded the fierc-est weapon that you can against her end-ing up in the backseat of some pimple-faced fellow's car. You win.

Day Fourteen Challenge: Cook Together

Roll up your sleeves and tie on the aprons. With your daughter, cook something together. It could be something as involved as an entire meal or something as simple as cookies or brownies. Learn from one another new skills in the kitchen, and take advantage of the time to talk to your daughter while your hands are busy.

Checklist

O Decide what day or evening you'll cook together. List your menu and what groceries you'll need.

O Gather all that you'll need for your cooking time (you may even want to grocery shop together).

O Put it on the calendar!

O Cook and eat.

Day Fifteen

Sweep the Garage

One trip to a video store, a mall, or even through a grocery checkout lane, and you will immediately realize that a war has been waged against one of your daughter's most precious assets: her sexuality. Sexy, glossy, and emaciated images of young women appear everywhere before your daughter communicating one strong message: *If you aren't sexy, you aren't anything.* The war is insidious and unrelenting. In fact, from where I sit, the fight for your daughter's sexuality is the most dangerous issue she will face during the years that she is under your roof. Here's why I say this.

> The fight for your daughter's sexuality is the most dangerous issue she will face during the years that she is under your roof.

In the 1970s, physicians contended with two primary sexually transmitted infections: syphilis and gonorrhea. By the 1980s, herpes reared its head in full force and between 1980 and 1990, herpes type 2 increased 500% in the United States. By the turn of the century, America counted more than thirty sexually transmitted infections. The most devastating part, however, is that of the more than twenty million new infections that occur every year in the United States, half are in our young people college-age and under. For an extensive discussion and bibliography, please read Chapters 1 and 5 in *Strong Fathers, Strong Daughters*.

The war against your beautiful girl is real and well-funded, and it isn't going away. Only one generation ago teenage girls felt that they had a choice about whether or not they wanted to have sex before they finished high school. Today, that's different. Girls tell me that they don't feel that they have a choice about sex. It's something that they have to do before they graduate, they say, because the pressure is everywhere. Saying *no* gets tiring.

Dad, You Make the Difference

This is frightening stuff, but here's the great news: you are the antidote. You, Dad, are a natural fighter, and when it comes to making sure that your daughter develops a healthy sexuality, you are the one in charge. Yes, you are more important than any high school boyfriend, you have more power than thousands of music lyrics, and you wield a greater influence over her sense of self than any glossy magazine cover. This is a sobering truth, but you can handle it. When it comes to defending and protecting your daughter, your natural juices start flowing, and you have everything that you need to keep your daughter healthy.

> Watching your daughter being collected by her date feels like handing over a million dollar Stradivarius to a gorilla.
>
> —*Jim Bishop*

Many fathers know that trouble surrounds their daughters but squirm when it comes to talking to them about sex. This is natural because you feel a healthy modesty about yourself and your daughter. What you need to know is that in order to influence your daughter's decisions about sex, you don't have to be an expert on infections, birth control, or the vocabulary that teens use. All you need to have is a strong desire to help your daughter navigate a toxic sexual culture, understand that her view of the sexual landscape is very different than a teenage boy's (and as a male you understand his view better than she), and be willing to have some uncomfortable but not excruciating conversations.

When your daughter is a toddler, tell her that her body is beautiful and precious. Tell her that she wears a bathing suit to the beach because when things are special, we keep them private. As she grows older, show her respect by giving her privacy in the bathroom. When she starts grade school, tell her that she will hear kids say things about moms and dads that she won't understand and that when she hears them, she should come and ask you because you are the grown-up with answers. When she's in middle school, check out the sex education program in her school and use it as a springboard for discussion. Ask her what she thought about what she heard.

Set Expectations and Rules

Most importantly, during her high school years encourage your daughter to have boys as friends. Let's be honest, rarely do good things come from high school romances. Most high school girls end up hurt and confused after breakups with high school boyfriends. We put far too much emphasis on dating, and girls get to know boys much better when they remain friends.

If you choose to let your daughter date, make a few rules. Your daughter will fight you on them but underneath she will feel like a queen because she knows that her dad loves her. When a boy comes to pick her up, make him get out of the car and shake his hand firmly. Making eye contact with him when you shake his hand sends a strong message: *mess with her and you mess with me.* Then smile.

When she comes home, be awake. Greet her to let her know that you have her back. My husband used to sweep the garage when our daughters were out at night (even with other girls) in order to greet them. He wanted them to know that he was always in the wings, waiting, aware and ready to aid them if trouble reared its head.

Day Fifteen Challenge: Give Her a Token of Your Love

Even though some cynics say that a piece of jewelry doesn't help a girl delay having sex, I beg to differ. Giving your daughter a visible symbol of your love, esteem, and expectations for her can have a powerful effect on her decision-making, especially in the heat of the moment.

Choose a ring, necklace, or charm bracelet for your daughter to wear as a visible reminder of your esteem of her, your expectations for her, and her commitment to wait before engaging in physical intimacy.

If your daughter is younger, give her a special piece of jewelry, but use more age-appropriate language when describing that she's "Daddy's girl."

Checklist

O Choose a piece of jewelry with a meaningful decoration—possibly an engraved message, a symbol of your faith, or an icon of something that is important to both of you.

O Plan a special date and time to present it to your daughter (a "non-conflict" moment is best; you may choose it as a gift for a birthday, a holiday, or to mark a faith journey milestone).

O Put it on the calendar!

O Present it to your daughter during a private moment, expressing your love for her. Instruct her to keep it as a special reminder of all that she means to you.

SECRETS
EVERY
FATHER
SHOULD
KNOW

SECRET 6

Pragmatism and Grit: Two of Your Greatest Assets

You are the voice of reason in your daughter's life. You establish and bear the standard for your family. You, Dad, are an expert problem-solver, full of practical wisdom, ingenuity, and determination.

Your daughter needs you to make her tough.

Establish a Moral Code
Examine the moral code that you want for your daughter. Write down what you believe is right behavior and wrong behavior.

- What's right:

- What's wrong:

- How to tell her my expectations:

Read Chapter Six, "Pragmatism and Grit: Two of Your Greatest Assets," in Strong Fathers, Strong Daughters.

Day Sixteen

Grit Gets Passed On

Your daughter will learn many lessons from you. They will be deeply imbedded in the woman that she becomes, and they will affect the profession she chooses, the man she marries, and how she perceives herself. Part of you will become part of her, and she will carry you for the rest of her life.

Since grit is one of your strongest assets, make sure that she carries this with her. Who else in her life can show her how to endure criticism, stay in college when she feels like a failure, or stand by her husband's side when he is diagnosed with prostate cancer? Her teacher won't. Her brother probably won't. But you can because you know how to rise to tough situations and get through them.

Teach Her to Stand Strong
Many fathers worry about their daughters getting into trouble when they hit junior high or high school. You fear that she will get pregnant, run with the wrong crowd, or start drinking. And these are the beginning of your worries. One of the most important

lessons that you can instill in your daughter is the ability to figure out what she stands for and then persevere in standing for those things. Girls who believe in a moral code fare better in life. When a girl has a keen sense of what is right and wrong, she has a plumb line for her own behavior. And she knows what she should expect from others.

Our culture has failed our children miserably in this regard. Any moral code has dissolved to a point where we accept the most bizarre behavior as normal and "okay for others as long as they don't hurt anyone." When we fail to teach our daughters how to respect *others*—particularly their parents and other adults—we fail to teach them any respect for *self*. Without ethical standards, girls are lost—mentally, emotionally, intellectually, and most certainly, spiritually. And then they are vulnerable to get into all sorts of trouble.

That's why your daughter needs you at this particular juncture in her life. Even girls as young as two years old have an intuitive sense of right and wrong. So when you see her embrace a moral code, praise her for it. A five-year-old girl knows that she shouldn't yell at her mother. So when she holds her temper, praise her for it. Tell her that was the right thing to do. When she is ten and wants to say nasty things about a girl in her class, tell her not to and then tell her why. Don't be shy about articulating to her what you believe is right and wrong. You

> Daughters who live with a strong moral code live with a deeper sense of purpose. Once they realize what is good and right, they find a way to live according to that code.

can give your reason, but often daughters don't ask for one. They know that a moral code exists; they just want all the blanks to be filled in.

As your daughter matures into the teen years, there will be many things in her world, which you will readily identify as right and wrong for her. You will not want her to see certain movies because they are too violent. She may want to have sex when she is fourteen with her sixteen-year-old boyfriend. Aside from the fact that medically this is very unwise, you know in your heart that starting sexual activity at fourteen is wrong. Even when she is an older teen and young adult, she will want to know what you think is right and wrong because in her eyes, you are her authority. You didn't earn it; she freely gives it to you when she is born. That's why what you believe and tell her matters so much.

Daughters who live with a strong moral code live with a deeper sense of purpose. Once they realize what is good and right, they find a way to live according to that code. Furthermore, once they do so, they soon realize that the rest of their friends don't always live according to the same standards and life suddenly gets a lot harder for them. That's precisely why you need to teach your daughter to pull out the grit. She must learn to stand up to what is wrong, to live better than others, and to adhere to a higher standard. Others can tell her not to cave to pressures around her, but when you tell her, she listens. Don't be fooled by her demeanor. She listens.

Start children off on the way they should go, and
even when they are old they will not turn from it.
Proverbs 22:6

Day Sixteen Challenge: Plant and Tend a Garden

Gardening creates a lesson in endurance for the gardener. With your daughter, plant a vegetable or flower garden. You may choose to plant a few seeds in a container or herbs in a bed. Choose something that will grow in your climate and soil, and don't plant so much that you become overwhelmed at trying to tend to it. One tomato plant in a barrel or geranium in a flowerpot will suffice, if you feel that's what you and your daughter can handle!

Discuss with your daughter what it takes to be a consistent gardener: patience, attention to detail, and goal-oriented thinking.

Checklist

O Check your local conditions for the best planting times and what plants, flowers, or herbs grow best in your area.

O Decide what you'll plant and what type of container you'll need.

O Purchase or gather supplies: containers, potting soil, seeds or seedlings, gardening trowels, gardening gloves, watering bucket or hose.

O Decide on the day you'll plant with your daughter.

O Put it on the calendar!

O Keep a garden journal with your daughter. Take notes on a regular basis as to how your garden is growing.

When the Going Gets Tough, Dad Steps In

When I was a little girl, my father always told me, "When the going gets tough, the tough get going." One thing I knew when he said this to me was that *he* was tough. And I wanted to be just as tough as he was. In your daughter's mind, you are stronger, smarter, and tougher than any other man in the world. Maybe you don't feel like these things, but no matter, she does and that's all that is important when it comes to making an impression on her.

Many fathers are uncomfortable challenging their daughters. You know that you can be tough, but when it comes to expecting your daughter to be tough, that's another story altogether. It's easier to come down hard on a son and demand better behavior, but when it comes to your little girl, well, sometimes you just don't want to be so tough. I understand this. I saw my own father wiggle when my sister and I got out of line. Rules were clear for all four of us, but somehow my brothers seemed to be held accountable more frequently. The downside for us daughters when fathers do this is that we learn to believe that we can't handle as much as our brothers can.

Make Sure She Knows She Is Strong

One of the best assurances that your daughter will stay out of trouble as she grows older is to make certain that she knows that she is strong. Don't compromise on this lesson. When you set standards in your home then waffle when it comes to holding your daughter accountable to those standards, she feels weak. She perceives that you, who are tough in her eyes, believe that she isn't capable of being as tough. And once she gets the idea in her mind that she isn't strong, then she doubts her ability to make good decisions, to stand up for herself, and to say no when she needs to.

Don't let this happen to your daughter. Teach her that she is strong. When she does something that you told her not to, make sure that consequences are as swift as they would be if she were your son. You must never be mean, critical, or demeaning, but be firm. The payoff for her will be enormous as she matures because when you teach her that you fully expect her to take control of her behaviors and make good decisions, she learns that she is strong. If you believe she is, then she believes she is. Sadly, most girls grow into adults doubting their capabilities. More often, girls are too timid to assert themselves and take charge of situations because they fear that they will either fail or that people will think badly of them. Don't let your daughter grow into one of these young women.

It's easy to protect your daughter when she is young and in your home. But what happens when she's no longer under your watch and someone tries to take advantage of her? Imagine that your daughter is twenty-one years old, at a bar, and a smooth talking thirty-year-old tries to take her home. What would she say? Or imagine she is thirty and her boss is taking advantage of her kind heart and willingness to work overtime and refuses to compensate her. Would she have the courage to stand up to her boss?

You can't afford to wonder. Derek would tell you that. When his daughter, Marcy, was seventeen, she came to me because she was depressed. She had reason to be. Her twenty-two-year-old boyfriend was sexually assaulting her, unbeknownst to her parents. Marcy was a "nice girl." She didn't want to hurt her boyfriend's feelings. And, she was scared of him. No one knew that she was in this predicament. I encouraged her to tell her father. Her dad confronted the boyfriend and told him in no uncertain terms to stay away from Marcy. After the boyfriend left, her depression went away. When life gets tough, Dad needs to intervene.

Teach Your Daughter to Be Tough

There are many ways to teach your daughter to be tough. The first is by setting an example, like Marcy's father did. The second is by keeping high standards for your daughter and not letting her off the hook when it comes to keeping them. Don't worry; your daughter can take it. Finally, tell your daughter not to be afraid of being assertive. Have her practice it. Watch how she interacts with their friends. Does she get pushed around or bullied? Is she a people pleaser? If so, talk to her about not being afraid to act from her instincts and to stand up for herself. Not only will you have a tough daughter, but you will also grow closer to her in the process.

Day Seventeen Challenge: Go Rock Climbing

Conquering a physical feat can be a great way to understand the extent of one's strength in all areas of life.

Take your daughter rock climbing, either outdoors if you are an experienced climber, or to an adventure center with an indoor climbing wall. Encourage her as she climbs higher and higher. Challenge her to press through any obstacles or fear to reach the top of the rock.

Checklist

○ Locate the ideal place for your climb. If outdoors, plan the day and time for your trip. If at an indoor facility, make reservations.

○ Put it on your calendar!

○ Day of the climb: If outdoors, bring appropriate snacks and water. If indoors, bring extra money for facility fees and snacks.

Day Eighteen

When Not to Back Down

There is delightfulness to male thinking that most of us women lack. That is, you are problem/solution-oriented thinkers. We women, on the other hand, think of five problems all at the same time then quickly turn our thinking into what we did to cause each of them. You, on the other hand, size up a situation, define the problem, and then propose a solution. Many of us women hate this because very often we don't want to hear the solution; we're still trying to figure out how we're to blame for the problem.

Your ability to problem solve without getting emotionally caught up in the problem can be a great help to you in your relationship with your daughter. Specifically, you can see things going on in your daughter's life that her mother may not be able to see. And, since you don't immediately identify with your daughter in any given situation because you are male, you have the advantage of responding to problems she faces in a much less entangled manner than her mother may.

Stand Up for Your Beliefs

The difficulty for you as a father comes in enacting the plans that you feel are necessary for your daughter. If she faces trouble at school, you may have a clear sense of the problem at hand but may back down when it comes to implementing a solution because you feel less qualified. After all, you are male and you don't always "understand" the situation, you are told.

One of the most common places that I see great fathers back away from standing up for what they believe is right for their daughters stems around clothing. Young girls want to dress like their friends at school and you know what that means—wearing skimpy, tight, and sexy clothing. I have had girls as young as five come into my office wearing bras and thong underwear. What really bothers me, aside from the grotesque inappropriateness of their underwear, is the fact that most often their mothers are well-educated and reasonable. When I ask why their daughters wear bras, their response is always the same, "Because that's what girls in her class wear."

Here's where you come in. You know better. You don't succumb to peer pressure from other mothers who dress their young girls inappropriately. In your mind, this is your beautiful little girl and you know the boundaries, which should be placed around her wardrobe. The issue isn't complicated and the fact that other girls in her class dress in a skanky manner doesn't mean anything to you. The issue feels far more complicated to her mother because she worries about your daughter feeling rejected by her friends.

In second grade, clothing isn't such a big issue; but in high school, it's huge. How many times have I heard of a daughter walking out the door to school when Dad stops her, telling her to change into more appropriate clothes? What usually happens next is that her mother chimes in and says that all girls dress that way. Then she asks her husband to leave the daughter alone. Off the girl goes to school.

You know as well as I that when it comes to parenting your daughter, particularly as she gets into her teen years, your opinion is often overruled. The argument is that you don't understand girls. So you turn from your instincts and shrug your shoulders. Don't do this.

Pragmatism and grit are two of your greatest assets, so use them. You think pragmatically and find problems that your daughter has. Clothing choice is only one. Your good sense tells you what others are. Sure, she has many, and wise fathers never battle all issues at once. But I'm telling you to never walk away from the battle. You know what's good and right for her many times, and you need to articulate that. She isn't mature enough to know what's best for her, and very often we mothers are blinded by identifying too closely with our daughters.

When you stand up for what you feel is right for your daughter, you may feel like the enemy in your home. Oh, well. You know better than that. As long as you implement rules for your daughter in a firm, loving, and respectful way, you will win her in the end. Where fathers get into trouble standing firm in rules is when they become critical, overbearing, and angry. You never need to be any of these with your daughter.

Parenting is gritty stuff. The good news is that you have exactly what it takes to parent your daughter very well.

Day Eighteen Challenge: Teach Her to Handle Money Responsibly

One pragmatic skill your daughter needs is money management. Our culture does little to encourage wise stewardship, debt avoidance, or living within your means. But your daughter needs to learn these lessons now.

Even if you need some help with this skill yourself, I highly recommend you and your daughter work on the family finances together. Allow her to evaluate income versus outgo and how well the family's budget balances.

Help her set up checking and savings accounts and get a part-time summer or after school job. Guide her in saving for a car and/or college. Give her common-sense money management skills early. (For more information and a comprehensive library of resources on this topic, consult my friend, Dave Ramsey's website, at www.daveramsey.com).

Checklist

O Gather supplies you'll need to teach your daughter about money management, which may include computer software, paper, pencils, calculator, resources by Dave Ramsey, etc.

O Decide when you'll go with your daughter to open checking and savings accounts. Put it on the calendar!

O Plan to work with your daughter at least once monthly to review the family (and her) budget. Put it on the calendar!

SECRETS
EVERY
FATHER
SHOULD
KNOW

SECRET 7

Be the Man You Want Her to Marry

Women are drawn to what they know. The man your daughter chooses to marry will undoubtedly be a reflection of you—whether for better or for worse.

Your Top Five
- Write down the top five qualities that you want in a son-in-law:

- Why do you believe these are important?
- Now decide how you will teach these to your daughter. What men do you know who exhibit these qualities? Make a point of remarking on these qualities in these men and tell your daughter why you feel they are important. Then, tell her to be sure to look for these same ones in men when she is old enough to date.
- Repeat this exercise often. One day you'll find that your list of five became her list of five.

Read Chapter Seven, "Be the Man You Want Her to Marry," in Strong Fathers, Strong Daughters.

The Longest Ten Yards

One day—sooner than you think—you and your little girl will be at one end of an aisle staring at a man who looks like a boy to you. She will loop her arm through yours, and memories will flash in your mind. You will see her riding a two-wheeler without training wheels or see the expression she had on her face after she landed the lead in the school play.

How did you get here? A lump wells in your throat and suddenly you are frightened. Will the man you see at the other end of the aisle really be good to her? Will he work hard for her or will his eyes roam to another woman one day? You press the thoughts from your mind and ask if she's really sure if she wants to do this. It's not too late, you say. You grab her hand and hold it tight.

If you haven't taken this walk, you need to get ready because you—more than anyone else in her life—have influence regarding the man she chooses, period. The man standing at the end of the aisle will reflect many of your successes. He may have your sense of humor or your passion for family. He will treat her the way you have treated her and her mother. Now is the time that you need to be asking yourself some tough questions so that you can assure yourself that he will be a great man—one who reflects the best of your character.

The million-dollar question is, *How do you do that?* You may wonder if you are up to the challenge. What about your faults? Will they be evident in his character as well? The truth is, they may be, but as long as you get the big stuff right, his good qualities will overshadow his bad ones. Certainly, you can get the big stuff right. You can help her find a man who will adore her, treat her with the respect, be faithful, and stick with her when life beats him up. You *can* do that for her.

Here's where you start. When she is young, let her know how she should be treated. When a girl begins to date a boy, she compares his behavior to her father's. If you never swear, then the moment her boyfriend does, she will wonder what's wrong with him. He will move down a notch in her mind. On the other hand, if she is used to you criticizing and yelling at her, she will expect her boyfriend to do the same.

Daughters learn to be comfortable in relationships, even if there is pain involved. Girls who are abused grow up to be abused by their boyfriends and husbands—not because they consciously seek this out; but rather because they gravitate to what is familiar. A powerful psychological phenomenon encourages girls to repeat what they know, not what they want. That's why a daughter who hates her father's bad qualities and swears that she will never put up with more of the same once she is married will end up marrying a man who treats her exactly the way her father did. I see this over and over. The good news for you is that this dynamic works for *all* of a father's behaviors. If an abused daughter seeks out an abuser, then how much more will a daughter who is cherished seek out a man who will adore her?

In a very real sense, you supply her with a gravitational pull. You decide what type of treatment from a man your daughter finds comfortable. What gravitational pull are you supplying for your daughter? Is your little girl so used to being respected and loved that if a boyfriend mistreats her she will walk out in an instant? Does your daughter demand that men respect her to the point where she would not tolerate verbal, emotional, or physical abuse? If your daughter said to a man, "My dad would never treat me that way," what would she mean?

Make sure that you can answer these questions. The best way to do this is to take a hard look at the words and the tone of voice that she hears you use. Equally important, examine how you treat her mother. Does your daughter see you stick by her mother's side, help and encourage her, or does she see you give up or talk down to her? The way you answer these will give you a preview of what her husband will be like.

Day Nineteen Challenge: Have Fun Together

Take your daughter out for some fun. Go bowling, roller-skating, to a zoo, to an amusement park, or to any other place that offers a get-away from your regular routine. Take photos of your time together.

Checklist.

O Decide what activity you'd like to do with your daughter.

O Check the hours of operation and admission prices.

O Put it on the calendar!

O Pack your camera, money for snacks, and have fun.

Day Twenty

Seeking Strong Character

When girls begin to date, they become enamored with very peculiar things in young men. Some admire boys who are tough and careless, believing that these characteristics represent courage. Other girls like boys who are athletic, not because they are disciplined on the field, but rather because other people watch them perform and admire their abilities. Some girls like boys who have nothing to do except spend time listening to them. They believe that these boys listen well, not because they are bored, but because they are compassionate. In other words, what young girls see in young men may be skewed by their immaturity. When your daughter begins to date, she may see a boy not for who he really is, but for who she wants him to be. That's why you need to be looking over her shoulder.

One of the most embarrassing moments in my life occurred when I was twenty-one. I was dating a fellow, and my father saw something in him that I couldn't see. He saw ulterior motive beneath his polite demeanor, and I was blinded by my desire to think he was nice. When the young man brought me home after a date and walked into our living room, my father literally ran him out. He told him that he was not welcome and that he was never to show up near me again. I was mortified. I didn't speak to my father for three days. After all, I reasoned, at twenty-one I was a grown woman, able to date whom I pleased.

Dads See What Daughters Can't

Months later, I learned this man had not only one other girlfriend beside me, he had two. How could I be so blind? When I found this out, of course, I refused to tell my father. I didn't want him to feel satisfaction after he had humiliated me in front a man— even if that man was a creep. When daughters date, they see boys differently than they really are and usually, if a father is paying attention, he can see what his daughter can't.

Whether your daughter is fifteen or fifty, the moment she gets enamored by a man, you need to help. Infatuation does something to the brain. It makes it dull in some ways and the problem is, the enamored one doesn't realize this. Helping daughters navigate dating is no easy task. For one reason, she will insist that you mind your own business. You are male, and she, therefore, believes that there is a lot that you don't understand about her and about love. Second, since she is feeling very independent, she doesn't want you to squelch that. She wants you to help but not suffocate her. She wants your wisdom but she doesn't want interference. But mostly, she wants to believe about a boy what she wants to believe. You and your wisdom threaten those beliefs and that frightens her.

> Let her know that you believe in her own character and that she should never lower her expectations when it comes to great character in the men she dates.

So be gentle, but be firm. Teach her when she is young what character qualities she should look for in a man. Pick five top qualities in men that you feel are crucial and then let her know what those five qualities are and why you think they are important. Help her become attracted to men who have depth and strong character. You can do this by pointing out great qualities in men when you see them, whether those men are friends, teachers, or family members. Because she looks up to you, she will remember these and when she begins to date, subconsciously, your list will drive her choices in men.

Many fathers feel intimidated when it comes to dating and their daughters. Don't be. Some fathers feel that dating is not their territory. Yes, it *is* your territory because you are the primary influence when it comes to your daughter's choice in boys and men. So don't back away. When you teach her, don't be demanding or condescending, but teach her in a way that communicates to her that you have every confidence that she will make good decisions. Let her know that you believe in her own character and that she should never lower her expectations when it comes to great character in the men she dates. Not only will this build her confidence in herself, it will assure you that she will pick good men.

---

*The words that a father speaks to his children
in the privacy of home are not heard by the world,
but, as in whispering galleries, they are clearly
heard at the end and by posterity.*
—Jean Paul Richter

Day Twenty Challenge: Bike Together

Go on a bike ride with your daughter. Choose an afternoon when the two of you can spend a few hours together just enjoying the sunshine and fresh air. Choose a café or small restaurant as your destination. Enjoy a refreshing drink or ice cream before you return home. Use this time to talk with her about the kind of man you want her to marry.

Checklist

O Decide on an afternoon for a bike ride. Check the weather forecast and both of your schedules.

O Put it on the calendar!

O Map out a biking route to a small café, restaurant, or ice cream shop.

O Make sure the bikes' tires are full of air, and fill your water bottles. Strap on your helmets and ride.

Day Twenty-One

Undaunted Courage

Raising a daughter is like having your heart leap from your chest and walk in front of you. Many times you want to reach out and put it back in so that you can keep it safe from those who want to crush it. But you can't. And neither can you lock your precious daughter in a room and protect her from all of life's hurts.

But there are things that you can do to help secure a good future for her. Fight for her life. Sometimes you will do this quite literally, but more often you will do it in more obtuse ways. Fathers often forget that most of the battles they wage for their daughters aren't the obvious ones. You may not have to drive boyfriends out of the house, reprimand a coach, or work your tail off providing college funding. Fights for your daughter will be right in front of you, but you won't recognize them.

Show Her a Good Marriage
You need to be the front warrior for your family. I say this be-cause studies show (as outlined in my book *Strong Fathers, Strong*

Daughters) that the best way to keep your daughter from all of the bad stuff in life is to help her have a good relationship with you. We also know that one of the best things that a father can give his daughter is a good relationship with her mother. Here's where the going gets gritty. Raising your daughter to choose the best paths in life (including finding a healthy mate) demands that you, Dad, show her what a good marriage looks like. Many husbands strug-

> Daughters worry about their parents when they see strife, and they can't concentrate on their own lives.

gle with wives who berate them or demand unreasonable changes. Some fathers find themselves home alone and separated from their daughters after their wives walk out. Many of you are raising stepdaughters or nieces, and you have moved into very challenging relationships with their mothers. Whatever your situation, you may endure difficulties, which stem from issues that you have had with your daughter's mother. The good news is that, even in the midst of it all, you can do what is right by your daughter.

Very often men who have been hurt by women retreat from them. When they do, they also retreat from their daughters. You can't do this. Whatever your difficulties with your wife, go to battle for the relationship with your daughter. Fight for your life to make your marriage stronger. I know that this is tough, but your daughter needs to see you refuse to surrender. She needs to see undaunted courage from you when it comes to the health of your family because this gives her security; it steadies the ground beneath her. Daughters worry about their parents when they see strife, and they can't concentrate on their own lives. Some girls begin to parent their mothers; others simply emotionally distance themselves from their parents and turn to peers, drugs, or sex to forget about pain at home. That's why you need to take on the burden of helping the family pull through difficult times. When you do this, your daughter can relax and go back to being a child.

When your daughter is a wife and mother, you want her to be with a man who will fight for her and for his marriage. I guarantee that when she sees you being faithful to her mother, loving her, and refusing to give up on your marriage, she will never settle for a man who will do anything less. And if you have a good marriage, she can still see you fight to keep it that way. Let her see you work to please her mother by serving her and doing whatever it takes to make her life better. Good men teach daughters how to seek other good men.

Examine Your Motives

Many fathers pride themselves on working hard in their professions or jobs. Others gain a sense of worth through community service or athletics. Think about the amount of time and energy you spend pouring yourself into things outside of your family. Many of these are noble, but if you are honest, are they as meaningful as your family? Good men get caught up in their work far too easily. Certainly it is important to model a good work ethic to families, but many fathers aren't working hard just to do that. If they are honest, they overwork because it feeds their ego. They get out of balance easily. If you are doing this, reign yourself in. It takes a tremendous amount of courage because one of the hardest things a man can do is to examine his work and his behavior and be brutally honest about his motives.

> She needs to see undaunted courage from you when it comes to the health of your family because this gives her security; it steadies the ground beneath her.

Strong fathers know when they are working hard for the wrong reasons and have the strength to back off and turn more of their energies into building healthier relationships with loved ones. If you want your daughter to marry a man like this, be one.

Day Twenty-One Challenge: Treat Her Mother Well

If you are happily married, make a special effort to do something nice for your wife. Do that thing you know she'd love to do, even if it may not be your idea of a "good time." Or find a way to take some of the burden of her responsibilities onto your shoulders: drive carpool, fold laundry, or take the kids on Saturday so she can have a quiet day to herself. When you do, let her know that you are doing it because you love her and want to make her life better.

If you are not married to your daughter's mother but are on good terms with her, go out of your way to help her with a parenting issue or some other matter of practicality in your daughter's life. If you struggle to have a positive interaction with your daughter's mother, use this opportunity to rise above your frustration to focus on how you can serve her. Keep in mind at all times the great benefit you daughter receives when she sees you treating her mother well.

Checklist

O Decide what you want to do for your wife (your daughter's mother).

O Gather any tools or instructions you may need to accomplish this task.

O Put it on the calendar.

SECRETS
EVERY
FATHER
SHOULD
KNOW

SECRET

8

Teach Her Who God Is

Your daughter needs God.

As a human father, you'll inevitably fail your daughter. Both of you need a bigger, better father.

Your Beliefs
What do you believe about God as:

- Creator?
- Sustainer?
- Father?

Her Beliefs
Ask her:

- What do you think God looks like?
- Where do you think he is?
- Do you believe in God? Why? If not, why not?

Don't worry about "having all the answers" to questions of faith. If your daughter stumps you on a point of religion or theology, offer to research it and get back to her. Then do that. You may even want to schedule an appointment with a clergy person (or a Sunday school teacher or youth group leader) to discuss her questions.

Read Chapter Eight, "Teach Her Who God Is," in Strong Fathers, Strong Daughters, *paying close attention to the list of positive effects of faith on girls.*

Day Twenty-Two

Have the Tough Conversations

Sex, God, faith, and death. These are a few of the topics that are tough to talk about with our kids. My rule of thumb when it comes to hard conversations is this: In every married couple, one partner is a chicken. The other is an even bigger chicken, and the former is on when it comes to the tough talks with kids.

Sometimes, conversations are just hard. The reason they're hard is that they are important. We are emotionally invested in whether or not our kids believe in God, whether or not they have sex as teens, and what they know about death. These are important to us, and we want to get it right when it comes to communicating our beliefs.

When it comes to discussing God, I can say this. The more you do it, the easier it gets. But there are a few things that make the conversations easier.

Know What You Believe

First, figure out what you believe. It's hard to communicate something about which you are uncertain. This is frustrating for you and even more frustrating for your daughter. So settle the score. Do you believe in God and if so, why? What do you believe about his character? How did you come to learn this? If you do believe in God, what do you believe about Jesus? Did he really die on the cross and rise from the dead, or didn't he? And if he did, what difference does it make in your life and in your daughter's life?

For some dads, this is easy stuff; but for others, my even posing these questions raises hackles. In our country, we no longer openly dialogue about God and faith for fear that we will be offensive. But get over that. We're talking about your daughter and she deserves—no, *needs*—to know how you feel about such important matters. There are far too many girls who haven't a clue about God's existence, ready to ascribe their beliefs to many crazy things. Don't let your daughter be one of those. Sure, she'll make up her own mind one day; but as with all other things, she will make her decisions after you have built a foundation of knowledge from which she can work.

Be Authentic and Honest

It is also important that when you talk about God, you must be sincere. No phony, syrupy stuff. She won't buy it. The issue of God is far too important for her, and she'll be looking for authenticity from you. If you are hypocritical—saying one thing and behaving in a contrary manner—all you say is in vain. You can't tell her that God is forgiving and then hold a grudge against her. If you say that Christ died to take away our sins and to help us stop committing those sins and you have an affair on her mother, what will she think about Jesus? Does he help or doesn't he? The beauty and frustration for you with your daughter is that you can't pull the wool over her eyes when it comes to you and your faith. She will see it in you. Or, she will see your lack of faith. She will look for it so that she can figure out what is important to you and then try it out.

Be prepared. Read the Bible. Read the Torah. Get ready for questions and answer them to the best of your ability. Daughters ask marvelously complex and deep questions and you never want to feel threatened by those questions. If you know the answer, state it. And if you don't, tell her that you will find the answer.

When our kids were little, my husband read to them from C.S. Lewis's *The Chronicles of Narnia* series every night. One evening, our girls began asking my husband questions and our then five-year-old daughter asked him a question, which stumped him. She said, "Dad, if Eve was born before Jesus came and died on the cross, is she in heaven?"

It took him a few days, but he gave her an answer. She'll never forget the conversation, and *The Chronicles of Narnia* are hard-wired into her mind.

Love the LORD your God with all your heart and with all your soul and with all your strength.
—Deuteronomy 6:5

Day Twenty-Two Challenge: Read a Classic Story Together

Several classic stories are both awesome and engaging fiction, while also offering Christian truths in symbolism and allegory. With your daughter, read through *The Chronicles of Narnia*, *The Lord of the Rings*, or an updated version of *The Pilgrim's Progress* (for example). Choose a way to read these, based on your schedule and your daughter's age. Maybe you'll read aloud to her every night, listen to an audio version during a long road trip, or each of you will read the books separately then get together once a week to discuss the story. As a special treat, once the stories are read and discussed, watch the movie versions together.

Checklist.

O Decide which classic you'll read together.

O Purchase or borrow copies of the book.

O Decide how you'll read this: together or separate. Put it on the calendar!

O Decide if you'll discuss the story once a week together. Decide where you'll go, what you'll do, and what day of the week you'll meet. Plan to read a chapter a week and schedule a "meeting" with your daughter for that many weeks. Put it on the calendar!

O Once you're finished reading, rent the movie(s) to watch together.

Day Twenty-Three

For the Love of God

Many fathers don't want to talk to their daughters about God because they doubt one of two things: they either question God's existence or his goodness.

Maybe you have doubts about one or both of these. If you do, you aren't alone. Men, who have been beaten up by life, find themselves at some juncture turning from their own strength and looking outward to something bigger and more powerful. When they lose a home in foreclosure, a child dies, or a wife walks away, they quiet themselves and in deep, private moments, plead with a God for help. Some hear him answer. Some don't. Depending upon what happens after their pleas, they decide whether God exists or whether he doesn't. You have made that decision.

I have seen mothers die and leave grieving husbands and toddlers to mourn at their funerals. I have heard fathers weep at the bedsides of their children with cancer. Being privy to these painful moments has been an enormous privilege, and they have changed me. I know that God exists.

Tell Her that God Is Real

I have listened to dying children reassure their mothers that they will be okay because an angel visited them in the night and told them so. I held my own dear father's hand as he died. As he took his final breaths, he opened his eyes from a coma and looked up in amazement at something glorious. He saw something that I couldn't. We don't believe in God until we need him—until we scream and say, "Show yourself to me because if you don't, I won't make it one more day."

Here's the difference between your faith and your daughter's. She believes far more easily than you do. She hasn't been beaten up by life the way you have. So don't make her wait until she is desperate in order to believe in God. Teach her now that he is real and tell her why you believe that. If you've had tough times and come to believe, you don't have to share details of the difficulties that led you to him.

Just tell her that you have found him. Here's why.

She wants to know all about you and God. She watches to see if you pray. She scours your mannerisms to see if you are dependent on another, like him. Don't worry; when she sees that you need God, it doesn't make her think that you are weak. Quite the contrary, it makes her love you more because now she gets a double-dose of help. She gets you *and* God.

Tell Her That God Is Good

In Genesis, Jacob wrestled with God because he was angry and wanted answers. He, like many men, wanted to know where he stood with God; he demanded to know something of God's character. You know the rest of the story. He limped for the rest of his life because after he wrestled with God, his hip socket was hurt.

But he left the fight getting what he wanted. He learned that God loved him and that he was all powerful. Genesis tells us:

> So Jacob was left alone, and a man wrestled with him till daybreak. When the man saw that he could not overpower him, he touched the socket of Jacob's hip so that his hip was wrenched as he wrestled with the man. Then the man said, "Let me go, for it is daybreak."
>
> But Jacob replied, "I will not let you go unless you bless me."
>
> The man asked him, "What is your name?"
>
> "Jacob," he answered.
>
> Then the man said, "Your name will no longer be Jacob, but Israel, because you have struggled with God and with humans and have overcome."
>
> Jacob said, "Please tell me your name."
>
> But he replied, "Why do you ask my name?" Then he blessed him there.
>
> So Jacob called the place Peniel, saying, "It is because I saw God face to face, and yet my life was spared."
>
> —*Genesis 32:24-30*

If you find yourself doubting God's goodness, look back over the past two years and write down the blessings that you have been given. Where did they come from? Did you always deserve them? Once you reconcile that God wants to bless you just as he did Jacob, a new peace will come to you. You need that peace, not just for yourself, but also for your daughter. She, too, needs to learn from you that God is not only real, but that he wants to bless her in ways that you cannot. You, after all, are only human.

Day Twenty-Three Challenge: Tell Your Faith Story

Read the story of Jacob in Genesis chapter 32. Put yourself in Jacob's place. Bible stories aren't just about the characters on the page; they can be applied to us, too. As you read, go ahead and substitute your name there.

About what have you struggled with God? When did you struggle? How has that struggle changed you? You may want to journal your thoughts.

Talk to your daughter about a time when you struggled and how your own faith was strengthened. She will be amazed at your depth and encouraged by your faith.

Checklist

O Find a few quiet moments to read the Genesis passage from the Bible, collect your thoughts, and write them down.

O Put it on the calendar!

O Choose one night before bedtime or a long car ride to talk with your daughter and tell her about your faith.

Day Twenty-Four

Keep No Secrets

Author and speaker Ken Davis once made the statement, "Live with nothing to hide." Do you live this way, or do you find yourself putting money in bank accounts that no one knows about but you? Do you have an email account that you don't want your wife to see? Let's get tougher. Would your daughter think differently of you if she could read your mind? *Ouch.*

Our nature is to hide behaviors about which we are embarrassed. No father wants his daughter to look down on him. Every father struggles with hidden desires, and the natural tendency is to lock them away in a place that only you can see. The problem is, when secret wishes go to dark places, they grow in magnitude. They don't get hidden from you; they do just the opposite. They begin to occupy more of your thoughts and energy and before you know it, your secrets begin to control you. You don't control them. Hiding things from loved ones never leads to anything good. Ever.

The best and worst news is that you can't hide anything from God. This is good news because, as I stated, secrets always end up biting you in the back. Knowing that God sees every private letter and every hidden dollar and hears your secret thoughts forces you to do something about them. You either determine to keep them secret and ignore that he sees, or you refuse to stash the money and to have private email accounts, and when ugly

> If she has faith, she will have fewer secrets. If she grows up without a faith, she will learn that she can hide whatever she wants.

desires surface, you train yourself not to act on them. Having God know everything helps fathers because it forces you to either face the truth or reap the consequences of telling God you don't care.

Living With Nothing to Hide

Your daughter needs you to stay honest. She needs to know that you don't live with anything to hide because she knows that what you hide isn't good. It hurts. And that's why your daughter needs you to teach her about God. Because when she sees that you love him, she will love him. And once she learns to love him, she will learn that she can't run from him. He is everywhere and nothing can be hidden. If she has faith, she will have fewer secrets. If she grows up without a faith, she will learn that she can hide whatever she wants.

If you want your daughter to live with a sense of freedom and peace, give her God. Once she learns to live with a vibrant prayer life and a deep connection to God, she will learn to like herself. Her self-confidence will blossom because she will learn to live with a sense that she has no need to hide anything. Shame will not be able to take hold and tuck itself away in dark corners because God sees every dark corner.

God Sees All

Faith keeps girls living with strong integrity because it teaches them that they have no need to run from anything or anyone.

God sees all that they are, and he likes what he sees. When your daughter believes that she does not have to feel shame because God accepts her as she is, strength will emerge from deep within her being and give her confidence. And when she has confidence, she will stay away from all of the bad stuff in life.

Studies show that God is good for daughters. With God, girls are more likely to be psychologically and mentally secure. They stay away from sex, drugs, and alcohol, and they are less likely to be depressed. This is just the beginning of the list. I am convinced that much of the benefits of faith come from the fact that faith in God helps girls to understand who they are, to like who they are, and to live with a sense of openness and honesty. With God, girls don't live with anything to hide.

So, you may ask, why do you need to be the one to teach her to grow her faith in God? One very simple reason: you are the face of male love to her. You taught her to trust and to love. You set the stage for her, and it is through her love with you that she learned what to expect from other male figures in her life. And, while God is neither male nor female, we universally accept that foremost, he has male character qualities. Secondly, Jesus was male. Therefore, in your daughter's mind, if she wants to trust him, she needs to have experienced trust in other male figures.

> When you daughter believes that she does not have to feel shame because God accepts her as she is, strength will emerge from deep within her being and give her confidence, which keeps her away from the bad stuff in life.

This is no easy path for any father to take. Living without secrets and teaching your daughter to live this way as she nurtures her own faith in God takes years, not days. But you are in this for the long haul with her, and now is the time to start down this path.

Day Twenty-Four Challenge: Pray For and With Your Daughter

Ask your daughter regularly how you can pray for her, and then pray for her requests in her presence. Set aside time (daily, ideally) that the two of you pray to-gether. Allow your daughter to hear you ask God for forgiveness and healing. Teach her The Lord's Prayer and pray it together.

Checklist

O Choose a time to pray with your daughter and put it on the calendar!

O If you'd like, keep a small notebook of your and your daughter's prayer requests. Record the ways in which the prayers are answered.

Teach Her to Fight

Your daughter lives in an extremely toxic world that assaults her mind. She needs the skills and courage to call the culture, "enemy."

This week, look around at the images that your daughter sees.

- What movies does she watch?
- To which musicians does she listen?

Then, begin to ask her questions in an open-ended manner. Listen to her responses.

From her responses, figure out what she believes she must look like and act like in order to be accepted by her friends: Does she need to be thinner? Smarter? More athletic?

Her False Beliefs

Identify one false belief that your daughter has about herself. Then, tell her that you want to help her change that belief because it is harming the way she feels about herself.

If she is young, you can even make a game out of it. Tell her to write down one ugly thing she believes. Help her keep it simple. Then, have her say it out loud. Tell her that whenever you hear her say it, she owes you a dollar. If she simply feels it and doesn't say it out loud, tell her to be on her honor system and that she owes you fifty cents when she feels or thinks it.

Read Chapter Nine, "Teach Her to Fight," in Strong Fathers, Strong Daughters.

Day Twenty-Five

Put On the Gloves

Someone told me once that entering the mind of a teenager is like going into a bad neighborhood; you never want to enter alone. The same is true with the mind of a young girl. If you could step inside your daughter's mind, you would find a myriad of thoughts that would disturb you as her dad. You would find one negative, self-deprecating thought after another. These thoughts usually start around age nine or ten, and they don't leave until someone helps her get rid of them.

Why are they there? There are many reasons, but the primary one is that she lives in a world that teaches her that her value is in how she looks. If you have doubts, listen to the banter of many fourth or fifth grade girls. You will find that many already struggle with feeling fat, stupid, or uncool. Watch how they stand. Most cover their stomachs because they feel that they are

> Fathers do not exasperate your children; instead, bring them up in the training and instruction of the Lord.
>
> —*Ephesians 6:4*

fat. And certainly by the time they hit sixth grade, many girls have started to slump. They feel too tall. They look downward because they don't want anyone to notice them or their face. Everything about their body language says, "I don't like what I am, so please don't look."

These thoughts occupy the minds of all girls, not simply those who struggle with depression or low self esteem. They are there because our girls live in a world that doesn't like them very much. That's why your daughter needs you—to show her that the culture is crazy because it can't see how wonderful she really is. And even if it did give value to her great qualities, she would still need you to reinforce them. Most importantly, you must realize that although many self-contemptuous thoughts swirl in her head, what she really cares about is how you feel about her. You are in the perfect position to interrupt those thoughts and reverse them.

Train Her to Identify the Culture's Toxic Messages

This is what teaching her to fight is all about. You don't need to teach her to physically fight; you need to train her how to identify toxic messages that she receives about herself from her culture and then change them into healthy, appropriate ones. The battlefield is in her mind. At first, you may be afraid to enter, but don't be. It is wonderful, filled with surprises and very tender.

Your first job in helping your daughter fight is to figure out what she is thinking about herself. Deep inside, she has insecurities, which you want to tease out, but this will take time. She won't divulge her innermost feelings at first, so be patient. If you are persistent, you will begin to see how she perceives herself. Does she think that she needs to be cool to her friends? Does she think that she will be more popular and more beautiful if she loses weight? What does she have to do with her friends in order to be liked by them? What about boys; does she want their attention or does she enjoy their company as friends? These are the areas where you need to do some digging.

How do you start? There are a few tricks. Of course, you could simply ask and with some girls this works well. But if direct questioning won't fly with your daughter, you have many options. One of the best places to start is to find out what her friends think about themselves. You can simply ask, "I know that some girls your age worry that they are fat and go on diets. Are any of your friends doing that?" If she tells you that, yes, some are, that gives you a clue that weight may be an issue for her. She will naturally want to please her friends, and if they think that being thin is important, chances are excellent that she will, too.

The other way you can probe is to use magazine cover photos of movie stars and other celebrities. Show her a picture and ask what she thinks about the woman on the cover. Is she beautiful? Why does she think she's beautiful? You can ask what she thinks of the behavior of a popular actress or singer. Once she tells you what she thinks, let her know that you understand why she thinks that way. Then, gently tell her what you think and why. You can say something like, "Isn't it sad that she feels that she needs to be thin or sexy in order to feel that people will like her? Do you ever feel that way?" Then, listen to her thoughts. Teach her lovingly but firmly that she is beautiful deep inside. Compliment her on her inner beauty.

Once you get started, keep the conversations going as she matures. Don't stop with a comment or two. She needs constant reinforcement, and I can guarantee every time she hears you compliment her on her character, you stab the self-deprecating thoughts in their core. This is what teaching her to fight is all about.

Day Twenty-Five Challenge: Celebrate History's Heroines

Take your daughter to the library to explore the biography section. Find books about courageous, strong women in history. You may want to encourage your daughter to read about famous first ladies, civil rights' champions, and/or great women of the Bible.

Checklist

O Decide when you and your daughter can take a trip to the library together. Put it on the calendar!

O Bring home the library books and read. Make sure the house is quiet (all electronics are turned off!) so that the two of you can read separately but simultaneously.

O After your reading time, take your daughter for a soda or coffee break and talk about the books you chose and the women's contributions.

Day Twenty-Six

Let Her Know Who the Real Enemy Is
(hint: it isn't you)

Now that you have started to peek into your daughter's mind, the real work begins. You can see where she gets her beliefs about her value, and it is clear to you that they are wrong. But here's your problem: she thinks that they are right, and you are wrong. Yes, she wants to believe you and yes, you have enormous authority in her eyes, but if helping daughters were as easy as telling them something and changing their minds, we would be in trouble. We would have a culture of young women who are fickle and easily manipulated. The reason that the messages your daughter receives from the world around her are so harmful is because they sink in. They root in her young mind. You need a crow bar to extract them. It's a good thing that you are good with crow bars.

Even daughters as young as seven years old begin to think that maybe their fathers don't really know what they're talking about. Dads don't want to believe this, but again, we are living in a world that doesn't like you very much. Your daughter learns from television and movies that you, dear Dad, are a dunce. You don't understand life. What you really need is a thirteen-year-old son to instruct you about life. That's what she sees in the movies.

You need to train her to identify toxic messages that she receives about herself from her culture and then change them into healthy, appropriate ones.

Right out of the shoot, you have one strike against you. Your daughter gleans from life around her that you are very out of touch when it comes to understanding kids. She learns that life in her world is very different from life when you were a kid. The conclusion she reaches is that you are on "the other side." Her teachers, friends, and movie stars are smarter about life than you, and they are the ones who are on her side. You are on the opposing team. Even if you didn't do anything to deserve being on the other team, she perceives that you are there. She feels that as she grows older, she will partner with friends and those who understand her, and you will be the enemy.

Don't take this personally. You may not have earned the enemy status. I say, "may not" because some fathers do. When a father is mean, critical, and overly demanding, a daughter feels that he really is the enemy. If you live in this camp, make amends. Change your behavior. Stop being critical, and don't let your temper get the best of you and isolate you from your daughter.

Establish the Culture as the Enemy

The second most important aspect of teaching your daughter to fight is to establish that you are not the enemy. Her culture is. Those who propagate messages that she must be thin, sexy, and popular and act like a non-thinking person are the enemy. You are her ally. You always have been the ally, and now is the time when you must make sure that she knows this. How do you do this?

First, you tell her. When she encounters a difficult situation at school or with her friends, let her know that you will always be on her side. You have her back. Sometimes you simply have to say this to her and reassure her. You may think that this is obvious to her, but you can't assume that it is. Second, as you help her identify the toxic messages coming at her, let her know

> Your daughter's mind is very much a war zone, and she needs your help in winning wars.

why those messages are there. Teach her that they come from those who want her to open her wallet and buy their stuff. Movies aren't riddled with sex scenes that titillate the minds of pre-teens because they want to teach girls lessons. They exist so that she and her friends will buy tickets. The same is true with magazines, music videos, and other forms of popular media and culture.

When you show her the scheme behind the messages displayed in the media, she will begin to shift her views. Over time, she will come to believe that maybe you know what you're talking about after all. You don't want her money; they do. You don't want her to change and become something that she's not; they do. Girls love a cause, and many eventually jump on the bandwagon when they find out the ulterior motives of retailers selling them products laced with messages that undermine her as a woman.

Once she realizes that you are the ally, and her culture is the enemy, you have accomplished a very important feat. You have put the gloves on her hands.

Day Twenty-Six Challenge: A "Real Beauty" Scavenger Hunt

One of the challenges facing your daughter (and society at large) today is that much of what we see in the media is simply not real. Because large corporations are driven by profit, they manipulate images so they will sell. We are inundated with airbrushed and altered photos of models, so that we come to believe the ideal of beauty is actually a standard that doesn't exist.

Take your daughter on a "real beauty" scavenger hunt. Think of some beautiful things you know: the beach at sunrise, fireflies dotting the yard at dusk, a mother dog doting on her new puppies, etc. You probably have an idea of what your daughter regards as "beautiful." Allow her to take photos of the real examples of beauty. Encourage her to reflect on them when she's feeling pressured to measure up to the culture's ideal of "beautiful."

Checklist.

O Decide when and where you'll go for the "real beauty" scavenger hunt.

O Put it on the calendar!

O Gather your digital camera, fresh batteries, and make sure the car is full of gas.

Day Twenty-Seven

It's All in Her Head

The fiercest struggles that any of us face occur in our minds. The Apostle Paul compared his own mind to a battlefield. He did the very thing that he didn't want to do. If that is true for a grown man with strong spiritual convictions, how much more poignant is it for a young girl who doesn't know who she is or what life is really all about? She, too, will battle with ugly thoughts about who she is and what she should be. The fight is very much in her head, and we parents often minimize the intensity of the battle

> For I have the desire to do what is good, but I cannot carry it out. For I do not do the good I want to do, but the evil I do not want to do—this I keep on doing.
>
> —*Romans 7:18b-19*

because it exists in her mind. We are wrong when we do this. Your daughter's mind is very much a war zone, and she needs your help in winning wars.

Wage War and Win!

Whether she is eight, eighteen, or fifty-eight, your daughter's mind can behave as the enemy. Once one victory is achieved, another issue will rear its head and another war will be waged. So when she is young, help her to wage war and win. Help her identify unhealthy messages and feelings of self-contempt. Give her the gloves to fight and then show her how the battle is to be fought. There are some very specific ways to do this and to win.

When your daughter thinks a certain way about herself, her feelings become attached to those thoughts. For instance, if she thinks that she is fat, she will begin to feel fat. If she thinks that she isn't as smart as the other kids in her class, she will begin to feel and act dumb. Our thoughts and our feelings are very much intertwined. Sometimes it's even hard to tease them apart. When we change the way we think, we ultimately change the way we feel. That's why cognitive behavioral training works well.

If we learn to interrupt certain thought patterns and redirect them, over time, we will learn to feel very differently. Many good counselors do this for anxiety disorders. They help a person identify feelings of anxiety and the thoughts that trigger them. Then, they train patients to stop the thoughts that trigger the anxiety and redirect them. Eventually, the anxiety resolves. The power of the mind to affect our feelings is quite profound. That's what your daughter needs for you to do. She needs you to challenge her ugly thinking and redirect it into healthy thinking.

Your job as a father is to find the deepest and most harmful beliefs that occupy space in your daughter's mind and help her challenge and change them.

She must learn to take a belief like, *I am fat and therefore an ugly person* and replace it with, *I am a beautiful person just the way I am.* Over time, as she learns to do this successfully, she begins to feel like a beautiful person.

Every girl contends with false beliefs about herself. Your job as a father is to find the deepest and most harmful beliefs that occupy space in your daughter's mind and help her challenge and change them. You can do it. I have seen good fathers literally alter the course of their daughters' lives by teaching them to replace false beliefs with true ones. And your job as a good father is to always lead your daughter into truth. The best place to start this is in her mind because when truth takes root there, her world turns inside out.

Day Twenty-Seven Challenge: Play in the Yard

Play a game of pick-up basketball or kickball with your daughter. Or throw and catch softball, kick a soccer ball, or even pitch horseshoes, spin hula hoops, or play lawn darts. Spend some casual playtime with your girl.

Checklist

○ Decide when you'll play with your daughter; you may want to choose an evening after school/work. Playtime is a great way to de-stress after a long day.

○ Put it on the calendar!

○ Gather any things you may need (balls, gloves, etc.).

Keep Her Connected

How do you spend your time?

Take a time inventory of your days over the past week. Write down what you did each day.

How much time would you guess you spent watching television, working on your laptop, or talking on your cell phone while your daughter was home?

Sunday:

Monday:

Tuesday:

Wednesday:

Thursday:

Friday:

Saturday:

Unplug and Get to Know Your Daughter

Turn off your electronics for one half hour per night while your daughter is home. Find out one new thing about her this week during this time that you didn't know.

Make a conscious effort to develop a new habit of leaving work behind and really engaging your daughter when you get home. Practice "turning off" work and "turning on" your interest in your daughter.

Ask your daughter about her day. When she answers, make eye contact. Listen to her words. As she talks, let her know that you are listening by asking her a few follow up questions.

Read Chapter Ten, "Keep Her Connected," in Strong Fathers, Strong Daughters.

Day Twenty-Eight

Come in from Orbit

Highly ambitious, energetic, and intelligent men fall into a common trap when it comes to being with their families. Sometimes, they orbit their loved ones rather than engage them. I understand this. You become so preoccupied with the demands and stresses of work that it is hard for you to suddenly switch gears and listen to your five-year-old daughter demand justice for her kindergarten classmate who "borrowed" her three crayons and refused to return them.

Many wives don't help out either. We communicate to you that since you're always working, you don't "understand" what kids experience at home and you are, therefore, disqualified from giving advice. Thus, a vicious cycle begins where you disengage the family. You are preoccupied mentally, and we wives tell you that you don't always understand the goings-on at home; therefore we need to run the show. So you disengage more.

If this has happened with your daughter, stop the cycle. Come in from orbit and let your wife (or your daughter's mother) know that you intend to work on being more engaged. Your daughter needs you more engaged. So once you decide to do so, where do you start?

First learn to flip a mental "on-off switch." When you leave work to ride the train or drive your car home, take this time to reflect on your workday. Allow yourself a time to debrief. Then make a conscious effort to mentally file your concerns away until later in the evening or the following morning. Tell yourself that you have the entire next day to worry about how to solve the problems you left behind.

Then, begin thinking about home and your daughter's day. What did she do? Did she take an exam, attend play practice, or play in a big soccer game? How is her relationship with her best friend? As you focus on imagining what transpired during her day, you will have a much easier time really paying attention to her as you walk through the door of your home.

When you see her, give her a hug. If she isn't around, greet her when she comes home. She may need a time of debriefing as well, so give it to her. But later in the evening, go to her and ask about her day. If she isn't used to you really paying attention to her, she may balk at first. She may try to brush you off and act as though she doesn't want you to talk to her. Don't take it personally.

When daughters are used to their fathers' "orbiting" the family, they become comfortable living in their own world. So when you try to penetrate that world, she may be uncomfortable at first. But be gently persistent. When she goes to bed, go into her room and sit on the edge of her bed and tell her goodnight. As the weeks pass, she will let you stay longer. She will become more comfortable talking to you. Slowly, she will let you enter her world, but she will need time and test your patience.

> Come in from orbit and let your wife (your daughter's mother) know that you intend to work on being more engaged. Your daughter needs you more engaged.

Day Twenty-Eight Challenge: Take a Drive

Choose a beautiful, sunny afternoon and take a drive with your daughter. Listen to some favorite music (hers and yours!). Explore some back roads in your area or take the "long way" to a favorite state park. If you happen to be far from home when night falls, consider renting a hotel room for the night—wherever you are. Allow yourselves to have no agenda. Your daughter will love the spontaneity.

Checklist

O If your schedule is so packed that you don't have pockets of time when you and your daughter could just "drop everything" and go for a road trip, then choose a Saturday or Sunday afternoon for your drive and put it on the calendar!

O Make sure the car is full of gas.

O Gather your and your daughter's favorite CDs.

O Pack extra cash to buy snacks, meals, or a souvenir from your trip.

Day Twenty-Nine

Go Fish

Spending time in nature with your daughter accomplishes three very important things. First, it puts the two of you on more equal footing. You are not in your world and she is not in hers; rather the two of you are in unfamiliar territory. This creates a wonderful dynamic between the two of you. That is, you are a team. When you paddle a canoe smoothly in tandem, you enjoy a smooth ride on the water. When you pitch a tent, you lean on one another's help.

Second, spending time in nature separates each of you from the distractions of your daily routines. She won't spend time ignoring you by texting her friends (no cell phones in nature, please), and you won't be constantly preoccupied with work. At first, this sense of being separated from the "comfort" of your busyness may bother you. You might worry that the two of you will have nothing to talk about. You will worry that she may be so bored away from her friends that she will leave your time together completely unenamored with you. Don't worry about this. Your first hours together may feel awkward, but press through them. Don't worry about what you will talk about. The truth is, you can make great memories and talk very little. Remember, the purpose of being together is that you are communicating to her that you cherish her and you enjoy her company. And here's the great news for you fathers who are short on words: fishing is a great excuse to be silent. Too much chatter scares the fish away.

Third, being away from other loved ones, friends, and co-workers heightens your sensitivity toward her and hers toward you. When you are alone together, you will notice things about her that you never saw before. Pay attention to her facial expressions, her perfume, and her comfort or discomfort with herself. You don't have to remark on these things, but pay attention. Realize also that she will tune into your every move: your tone of voice, mannerisms, comfort with her, and your comfort being away from work. She won't let on that she's watching you with hawkish eyes, but she'll be doing it.

> When you are alone with your daughter, you will notice things about her that you never saw before.

My own dear father passed away three months ago with severe dementia. During his last years, I would sit at his side and hold his hands. Sometimes I sat with him in silence, hoping beyond hope that he knew that the hands that held his were mine. When I did talk, I reminded him of the days we spent in a canoe, floating on an inland lake in northern Maine, fly-fishing. My father was an introvert, and during our times in the canoe, hours would pass without a word exchanged between us. In a way, those moments were more precious than the times we talked. With each cast, I smelled the smoke from his pipe. When I cast my line, I ached for it to land as smooth and as straight as his did—right at

> Your daughter needs moments with the silence of nature surrounding only the two of you.

the tip of a trout's nose. I wanted him to notice that I could cast well, too.

Your daughter needs moments with the silence of nature surrounding only the two of you. Give her these experiences so that when you are old, she will have cherished times in her memory bank from which to draw. These will be the memories that change who she becomes as a woman, long after your time together has passed.

Day Twenty-Nine Challenge: Go Into the Woods

Take your daughter into nature. Your outing can be something as simple as a slow walk through your local park or something as involved as a weeklong camping trip.

Checklist

○ Determine a specific weekend, week, or just a day that you can take your daughter for a nature date.

○ Put it on the calendar.

○ Depending on what you decide to do, gather the supplies you'll need (such as canoe, fishing rods and tackle, camper, etc.).

○ Get directions and hours of operation for the place (such as park, campground, lake, etc.) you're headed.

There's something like a line of gold thread running through a man's words when he talks to his daughter. Gradually over the years it gets to be long enough for you to pick up in your hands and weave into a cloth that feels like love itself.
—John Gregory Brown

Day Thirty

Unplug

Your daughter wants you to know all about her. Even if she's fifteen, deep down, every girl feels special if her father knows what she likes to eat, how she feels, and who her friends are. Having someone whom we love and admire know us inside and out gives us security. It makes us feel a little less alone in the world. Have you ever had your wife get angry because you don't know what she wants? The women in your life want you to know them so deeply that you can anticipate their wishes and needs. And, of course, you should never have to ask what those are. If you love them, they believe, then you don't need to ask. This is tough for you and unfair. You're not psychic, of course. But you can pretend.

Part of the way your daughter feels loved is by having you know all about her. No, you can't read her mind, but you can learn more about her than you currently know, and I can guarantee that when you know more, she'll feel that you are interested because you love her. But there's a catch. She wants you to know more but not act nosey. She doesn't ever want to feel that you are digging for information because you are certain that you will uncover something bad. I see parents do this all the time with their kids, and it always backfires. Fathers are so sure that their daughters are up to no good, that they ask questions with a critical and accusatory tone. No daughter wants to feel as though you're trying to trap her, so don't. Make sure that any effort expended in knowing her better is done in a genuine and loving way.

So how do you do that? Very simple. Spend more time with her and do two things. Ask questions and listen. Fathers tell me repeatedly that their daughters refuse to talk to them. That's not true. Daughters will talk, but they will never open up if they feel that Dad isn't listening. If he *is* listening, but readies himself to pounce with directions about how his daughter needs to change, he can also guarantee he's just silenced his daughter. All daughters will refuse to talk if you do that.

But there's another problem fathers face when it comes to learning more about their daughters. Dads compete for their daughters' attention. And, if we're honest, she competes for your attention, as well. We live with too much electronic gadgetry, and many times, gadgets steal our attention. As helpful as technology is, it can also obliterate effective communication. I heard one of my patients refer to his father's smart phone as "the family killer."

> If you are going to learn more about your daughter and understand her world, you are going to have to unplug a bit.

If you are going to learn more about your daughter and understand her world, you are going to have to unplug a bit. There is no way that you will be able to have meaningful conversations with your daughter if one of you is plugged in. When she's texting, she's not listening to you. If your cell phone is always at your ear, you can forget learning anything about her. But if you make a point of unplugging, you can get her attention.

Is unplugging hard? You bet. For busy, ambitious, hard-working fathers, shutting your laptop and turning off your cell phone is a challenge. But you are good at doing hard things.

Studies show that kids spend about six-and-one-half hours per day with some form of media. I personally believe that the number of hours is higher when you now factor in using media for school use, not just for fun. You can bet that some of those six-and-one-half hours are packed with some pretty tawdry stuff.

Regardless, compare that to the amount of time that your daughter spends in conversation with you. How much time do you spend daily chatting with your daughter? Ten minutes? She's lucky if she gets a half an hour.

Now think about this. You know that she needs more of your influence than she does the influence of her media. Texting doesn't make her feel more loved; having you know who she is by spending time together does. Movies are entertaining, but the same amount of time spent with you changes the woman that she grows up to be. If you believe that these statements are true, then ask yourself, why does your precious daughter spend more time with electronic stuff everyday than she spends with you, her dad?

> The quickest way to help girls gain confidence and healing is by increasing the amount of time they spend with caring adults.

When girls in our community get into trouble, many spend time at a halfway home. As soon as these troubled girls enter the home, attentive adults watch them fastidiously. You could almost say that they become tied to them. We do this because we know that the quickest way to help girls gain confidence and healing is by increasing the amount of time they spend with caring adults. Girls feel loved when they know that an adult wants to be involved in their lives and know them on a deeper level.

Day Thirty Challenge: Solve a Puzzle

It's time to unplug. Turn off all electronic devices, including cell phones and laptops. Choose a quiet and slow-moving activity for the both of you to do together. Some examples include working a jigsaw puzzle, playing a game of chess or Scrabble,® or building a dollhouse (if you're handy with a hammer). Find something both of you enjoy and something that you can "stop" and "start," depending on your schedule.

Checklist

O Choose an activity to do together, and purchase the supplies you'll need.

O With your daughter, choose a start day and time. If you need to, set aside an hour or two each week to work together. Don't worry about trying to finish in any sort of timeframe.

O Put it on the calendar!

Final Thoughts

CONGRATULATIONS! You finished the challenge. You're done. Or are you? Could it be that you have just begun—I mean really begun—raising your beautiful little girl? Whether your daughter is two or twenty-two, you may feel that you are planting your feet on a path you have never walked. Others of you may be familiar with the path but needed encouragement or a bit of a reigniting. Wherever you are, you need to know that life with your daughter will be a continuous series of finishes and starts.

Just when you think you understand what it means to be the most important man in her life, you will feel like an imbecile. One day you are her biggest hero, the next day you are the only thing standing between her and happiness. That's what life is like with a daughter. You are smart, and then you are stupid; at least that's the way she makes you feel. So don't be fooled. These are her feelings; they are not reality. You are reality. Your character, your resolve, your patience, and the grace that you afford her are reality, but she just may not know it. The realities of who you are will never change, so hold onto reality and not your (or her) feelings.

As you move forward in your life with your daughter, remember that your days may be confusing. Some days you may feel that you don't know a thing about being a good dad. Don't be discouraged. What you have begun to learn in these lessons will never be wasted. The insights you have gained or the encouragement you have found will serve you well during those moments when you think you are starting parenting from ground zero. Be patient with yourself because the mere fact that you were willing to take this challenge proves that you have what it takes. You are in this relationship for the long haul. If life beats you up, you will be there for her. If life gets tough for her, you will show up and help her like no one else can.

Raising a daughter is unlike any other venture. Some months you will make great progress by helping her through a difficult phase, and then another trial may appear. Will you be able to draw on your past successes to help you through the next trial? Maybe; but maybe not. You may have to come up with a completely new plan. But you can do that. Come back to this place and take these challenges again. You will find that they will mean one thing when she is four and something completely different when she is fourteen.

Hold onto this text and put in on your shelf for a year or two. When your daughter is older, (particularly if she is going through a tough time) pull it out and do two things. First, read the notes you wrote to yourself during the challenge. Then, retake it. You will be amazed at your knowledge as a father and at the depth of understanding you have gained over the years. Finally, always remember that you are wired with everything that you need in order to be a great dad. Taking the challenge simply sets a spark to the wiring that is in you so that you will be reignited. I pray that *Strong Fathers, Strong Daughters: The 30-Day Challenge* will always be that spark for you.